JOSEPH COVINO JR

IMPOTENT COPS: AND THEIR *WEE WILLY* COMPLEX

EPIC PRESS

Published by:
Epic Press
PO Box 30108
Walnut Creek, CA 94598
First *Epic Press* Edition published 2009

FOR

WILLIAM R "NICK" CARTER,

FLORIDA
STATE TROOPER

EXTRAORDINAIRE

CONTENTS

PROLOGUE:

I
ASPIRED
TO BE

BURT REYNOLDS

AKA
"DAN AUGUST,"
TV DETECTIVE

COPS

together with a sweeping assortment of police and private detectives were amongst certain quarters at least hip, cool and all the rage in *1971*—despite all the race riots and agitating anti–war protest and counter–culture movements raging right alongside them!

Richard M Nixon led the nation as its reactionary and right–wing "law–and–order" president. Director William Friedkin's crime film drama, *The French Connection(1971)*, starring actor Gene Hackman(as pork pie hat–wearing New York City police detective Jimmy "Popeye" Doyle), would win five Oscars and become the first R–rated movie to win the Academy Award for Best Picture since the introduction of the *Motion Picture Association of America(MPAA)*film–rating system.

Broadcast television airwaves were inundated with weekly serial police show and detective dramas the likes of *Adam–12(1968–1975)*, *Cannon(1971–1976)*, *Columbo(1971–1994)*, *Dan August(1970–1971)*, *The F.B.I.(1965–1974)*, *Hawaii Five–O(1968–1980)*, *Mannix(1967–1975)*, *McCloud(1970–1977)*, *McMillan and Wife(1971–1977)*, and *The Mod Squad(1968–1973)*.

§

Such was the auspicious cop climate during my senior year at *Pensacola Catholic High School* throughout my graduation academic year of 1971–1972 once I entertained stupid notions of attending *Okaloosa–Walton Junior College*(founded in 1963)in nearby Niceville, Florida—a city in Okaloosa County located close to Eglin Air Force Base and previously known as the *Boggy Bayou!*—and noted for its reputedly excellent law enforcement program and police academy. In 1988 it metamorphosed into *Okaloosa–Walton Community College* and then again in 2003 into *Okaloosa–Walton College* after attaining four–year status. By just this past June 2008 it metamorphosed once more to *Northwest Florida State College* under a Florida College Pilot Project permitting several public community colleges to offer four–year degrees.

Today the college confers an Associate of Applied Science(A.A.S.)degree in so–called Criminal Justice Technology and vocational credit certificate programs in Corrections and Law Enforcement—Law Enforcement and Corrections Basic Recruit Academy programs. *NFSC's* a Florida Department of Law Enforcement certified program and the region's designated Criminal Justice Training Center as part of its so–called "Public Safety Division."

What's most relevant and telling is the college's current published online internet definition of **Criminal Justice:**

"The safety, order, and freedom of society depends on our criminal justice
professionals. These men and women are law enforcement officers, security officers,
detectives, investigators, deputy sheriffs, correctional officers, and public safety
administrators. Their job duties include investigating complaints, handling traffic
emergencies, arresting violators, overseeing people in jails and prisons, researching
information on suspected criminals, and issuing citations."

All very noble, high–minded, high–principled and high–sounding, isn't it? After being indirectly brainwashed and indoctrinated by so many made–up, make–believe and phony mis–portrayals by farcical Hollywood television and motion picture productions, appealing to my own scrupulous sensibilities, I fell for the fraud and bought right into all that bogus police propaganda!

§

So small wonder I suddenly aspired to be like fellow good old Florida boy and up–and–coming film actor, **Burt Reynolds**, playing perennially brooding but hip and cool Det. Lt. Dan August—the title character in the short–lived, Quinn Martin–produced ABC television network crime drama series about a police homicide detective working the crime beat in his fictional hometown of Santa Luisa, California(supposedly modeled after Santa Barbara, California though actually shot in Oxnard, Ventura County). The series itself was based on the 1970 made–for–TV movie, *The House on Green Apple Road*, starring Christopher George(Sgt. Sam Troy of *Rat Patrol* fame)as Dan August.

§

Once I called upon one of these so–called "Criminal Justice professionals"(a deputy sheriff to be precise), pleading for help to preserve my own personal "freedom" and "safety," I received a rather abrupt rude awakening by getting a strong, potent dose of fiction–busting reality!

11

ONE:

ABSCONDING

ABUSE

UNDER

THE

INDIFFERENT

OVERSIGHT

OF

THE

"LAW!"

*"The Escambia Sheriff's Office is dedicated to protecting the rights and safety of each and every citizen."—**Current Website, 2009***

Suffice it to say I was both repulsed and intimidated by my bullying step–father—one Clester Rolan Cheetham—who'd terrorized me as a kid for roughly the past nine years ever since I'd been forced to take up my abode with him and my mother for the fourth grade in 1962. We lived in a small cinderblock house at 605 Edison Drive in the stately–sounding *Mayfair Estates*, a working–class neighborhood in west Pensacola, Florida. For nearly a decade then I'd been to some degree a so–called "abused child"—another story altogether. Suffice it to say though that my loathsome *bastard* of a step–father, whom my high school band director once referred to as "roughshod," was to a great degree disturbed, violent and dangerous. Because of his overbearing bulk and manner I'd referred to him myself as simply the "big man."

When I attempted absconding from that severely dysfunctional "home" the year before at just 16 the big man—in characteristically fine form—had socked me hard in the mouth with his heavy–handed fist, knocking me down to the floor in front of my coldly indifferent mother, who sat rocking and nodding in her recliner, scoffing smugly, *"Good!"*

On that afternoon of my ultimate escape in 1971 I'd summoned at 17 the assistance of an Escambia County Sheriff's deputy from *Pensacola Catholic High School* at 3043 West Scott Street in the nearby neighborhood. A brave band buddy of mine named Pete drove me in his mustard yellow two–door, convertible *Chevrolet Corvair* coup to that hellish house to collect my belongings under the cop's supervision. Grudgingly the deputy sheriff followed us from behind.

Arriving at the scene I duly cautioned the cop—a dark, lean and slim middle–aged gent with short, closely–cropped and greying hair—that the big man had a violent pre–disposition and kept drawered in his bedroom a pair of handguns: a Beretta pistol and a .357 Magnum, which my mother would exchange later on for a .44 *"Dirty Harry"*–style Magnum revolver.

With my mother seated habitually in her living room recliner the big man met me at the side carport door.

"I've come to get my things," I told him simply, ushering Pete into the house right past him, "and I'm not going to be threatened anymore."

Caught off guard for once the dumbstruck big man—in one of his grandest, self–defensive gestures of phony–baloney hypocrisy—actually invited the deputy sheriff inside. Wisely the deputy sheriff declined and stayed standing outside on the carport doormat.

In the meantime Pete obligingly helped me tote out to his car my loaded trunk and several bags full of my things. I felt suddenly stressed; my head throbbed and my heart pounded. And the air in that house was suddenly stifling and charged with violent tension.

Finally the big man himself lumbered back into my rearward bedroom to hover over us and oversee our removal operation.

"I'm not taking anything that doesn't belong to me," I volunteered.

Abruptly the big man ordered me to surrender the payment book for my brand–new gray 1971 *Dodge Dart Demon* compact—for which I'd been paying entirely out of my wages from working as a clerk for the *Jitney Jungle* supermarket. Since the automobile was technically bought in my mother's name, insisted the big man, either he or she would have to continue paying the installments.

Since I'd already invested in the vehicle roughly $800 of my own money, I objected, I could continue making the $80 monthly installments.

"*Leave* it," the bullying big man snarled lowly beneath his breath, contorting his rageful and reddened face into the most grotesquely menacing expression he could muster.

"You're right," I said, nonchalantly tossing the auto payment book aside.

My indifferent bitch of a mother likewise ordered me to surrender the B–flat *Bach* model trumpet they'd bought me as a Christmas present during my sophomore high school year. Months later I'd find that trumpet in the used horn stockroom at *Monzingo Music Company* at 1410 North Pace Boulevard.

Inside I was overwhelmingly paralyzed with fear. Even with Pete in the bedroom and that deputy sheriff nearby outside I strongly sensed that the big man could've gleefully killed us all. Quite candidly that supervising deputy was way too shrimpy for my taste! So Pete resumed helping me haul off most of my remaining things.

"Well," I overheard the stupidly duped deputy sheriff sympathize with that bastard big man, who'd been suckering the cop with some concocted cock–and–bull story, "if you're having marital problems it's probably best the boy is leaving."

Freakin' fool! Marital problems! The big man had recently discovered that my mother had been screwing around with a hospital medical lab technician whom he'd already threatened to murder or have killed—Mafioso–style. In front of several onlookers at the supermarket where I worked he'd blatantly blustered that he'd "hurt" me as well.

Before Pete could finish helping me carry everything belonging to me to his car the deputy sheriff headed for his squad car.

"I don't see that you're in any danger here," the cop scoffed snidely. "I can't *waste my time* sitting around here."

"Stay just a little longer while we finish," I pleaded, pointing panicky at the big man who hovered over us from atop the sloping grade of the driveway. "*Look* at him! He's crazy!"

"Look son," the cop preached stupidly, "I can't solve your problems."

"I'm not asking you to solve anything," I protested. "I just want you to wait a little longer."

"I told you son," the cop rudely waved me off with a curt flick of his hand, "I've got *more important things* to do."

Yeah, like issue some traffic citations, no doubt!

I refused to go back inside that house unsupervised and unprotected. So I retreated with Pete with whatever belongings of mine we'd already salvaged and we promptly drove off to our next destination.

Sometime later on that inept deputy sheriff passed through my checkout at the supermarket whilst I was cashiering, buying a bottle of wine.

"How'd everything work out?" he asked me stupidly.

"Just fine," I answered back tersely.

No thanks to him—the freakin' fool—I was thinking! Thanks to him though I lost some dearly treasured things which I was forced by his deliberate dereliction to leave behind.

Sometime after that both the driver's door and the trunk of my brand–new *Dodge Dart Demon* compact had been badly bashed in once that disturbed bastard step–father had tried running off the road with his heftier *Plymouth Fury* my mother, who'd been driving my car in desperate flight across the elevated Mobile Highway "Circle" viaduct!

After living in that hellish house for nearly a grueling decade I'd safely and successfully escaped at last! And I'd encountered in the process my first perfectly ineffectual, utterly useless and profoundly ***IMPOTENT COP!***

TWO:

IMPROPER,

UNNECESSARY,

WASTEFUL

ARRESTS

*"Please be advised that you or your client, Mr. Covino, can pick up the record which we have **expunged** from our files concerning the above court order. This record cannot be mailed as a receipt has to be signed in order to complete our files."—**Chas. D. Grant, Chief Identification Officer, Escambia County Sheriff's Dept., Pensacola, Florida, 9 March 1976***

"Interfering(sic)With a Police Officer in his Line of Duty."

Or so read my subsequently expunged Escambia County Sheriff's Office arrest record dated Saturday the **8th of December 1973**.

Its final disposition as of Wednesday the **2nd of February 1974** the case was duly **"Nol Prossed"**: *"The deputy sheriff does not wish to prosecute any further. Therefore, evidence is insufficient to prove the defendant guilty beyond a reasonable doubt."*

§

Nolle prosequi is a Latin legal phrase meaning *"do not pursue."* It's the term used in many common law criminal jurisdictions to describe a prosecutor's application to discontinue criminal charges before trial, or up until but before verdict.

Generally the application to *"nolle"* or *"nol pros"* a case is made after the filing of an information or indictment: when the prosecutor representing the state's interest is of the opinion that an adjudication of the charges is not in the interest of the public and/or that the available and admissible evidence is insufficient to satisfy a jury beyond reasonable doubt.

In most circumstances the court with jurisdiction to hear the case must adjudicate on the application for *nolle prosequi*—thus finding the defendant not guilty of all charges. To determine where the public interest lies a motion for *nolle prosequi* indicates more often than not that the prosecution aspires to pursue the case no further(be it a civil and/or criminal case).

In essence under United States jurisprudence this motion is usually filed due to the defendant's innocence— hence *"innocent until proven guilty."* In a reasonable court of law a motion for *nolle prosequi* is granted only if it's concluded that the defendant is indeed innocent. In conclusion this means the prosecution knows it hasn't enough evidence(or *any* evidence)that a crime's been committed and must therefore consider the accused/defendant innocent. If new information comes to light or the circumstances of the case change during a given period of time—typically 13 months—then the charges can be reinstated.

§

In my special case the cops duly copped out! And with damn good reason! Evidence was insufficient to prove me guilty beyond even an *un*reasonable doubt. And I hadn't "interfered" with anybody—unless running off at the motor mouth for the length of a single spouted sentence could conceivably be considered "interference."

Late that Saturday night my own aspiring cop–to–be pal, **William R "Nick" Carter**, and I were leaving the so–called *Sahara Club* at about two–thirty in the morning when we witnessed the bar's brave, overgrown, brawling "bouncer" pinning down *face*-down on the hard gravelly ground some runty Navy swabbie—supposedly for trying to "steal furniture" from the dive's not–so–extravagant interior. Unless he was hiding it in his back pocket the swabbie wasn't packing any conspicuous club furnishings. From what we could see all he was really trying to do was peaceably leave the club property.

Warrington, where the club was located, is a census–designated place(CDP)in Escambia County situated some six miles southwest from Pensacola, Florida that includes the *Naval Air Station(NAS)*—home base for the United States Navy Flight Demonstration Squadron, the six–pilot, precision–flying aerial demonstration team known as the *Blue Angels*. So the community was a sailor's stamping ground and the club a sailor's hangout.

So once Escambia County Sheriff's Deputy, **James A Weaver, Jr**, arrived on the scene to rashly make his snap judgments about the incident, taking the compliant swabbie into custody, he naturally outright ignored my dispassionate attempt to explain—from a discreet distance—what we'd witnessed.

"Hey buddy," I called out to the seized swabbie, "you ought to sue them for false imprisonment!"

That's when Weaver laid firm hold of my hand and seated me in the back cage of his squad car as well—driving us to the Escambia County jail where my pal, Nick, would pay a $150 bond to bail me out!

Nick nearly persuaded Weaver to release me without charge but Weaver was afraid of "repercussions" from his false arrest. So he felt compelled to carry out the charade to its illogical farcical conclusion.

"Interfering with a police officer in the performance of his duty."

So read Weaver's "charges" in his first sworn "Affidavit of Complaint."

At arraignment the bogus charges metamorphosed to *"resisting arrest without violence."*

Before it was all over it metamorphosed yet again to *"obstruction of justice."*

I was coerced as a clueless kid into executing this whitewashing affidavit:

"I, Joseph Covino, Jr., hereby state that Deputy James A. Weaver, Jr., was engaged in the lawful execution of a legal duty on the 8th day of December, 1973. And I hereby stipulate that it appeared that Deputy Weaver

*had probable cause to arrest myself for obstruction of
legal process on said day, and in lieu of prosecution of
said arrest of myself, I further stipulate that I shall not
bring legal action against Deputy Weaver nor anyone
else in the Sheriff's Office of Escambia County, Florida."*

So I'd copped out as well even though in retrospect I
should've been the one suing Escambia County for false
arrest and false imprisonment!

Long story short: through motions instigated on my
behalf by Pensacola's Public Defender, **James Ron
Shelley**, First Judicial Circuit, my lame–ass arrest record was eventually duly and legally **expunged!**

§

In the common law legal system an expungement
proceeding is a type of lawsuit in which the subject
of a prior criminal investigation or proceeding seeks
that the records of that earlier process be sealed or de-
stroyed, thereby restoring the subject's name. If suc-
cessful the records are said to be **expunged!**

While expungement deals with an underlying criminal record it's a civil action in which the subject is the
petitioner or plaintiff asking a court to declare that the
records be **expunged!**

Each jurisdiction whose law allows **expungement**
has its own definitions of **expungement** proceedings.
Generally **expungement** is the process to "remove
from general review" the records pertaining to a case.
In many jurisdictions though the records may not completely "disappear" and may still be available to law enforcement.

*"Enclosed is a copy of the Florida Statute which
relates to expunging a criminal record,"* **Miriam M.
Ptomey**, Assistant Public Defender, wrote me in her

letter dated **10 December 1976**. *"This statute allows a person after an order of expungement is entered to answer '**no**' to the question, 'have you ever been arrested?'"*

§

Upon my release on bail the night I was arrested some smart–ass impotent cop cracked, "Come back and see us again sometime—*slick!*"

Nearly three years later to the day I did indeed go back to the Escambia County Sheriff's Office: to pick up in person my record for an improper, unnecessary and superfluous arrest which *Slick* himself successfully **expunged!**

§

Quite honestly I felt precious little animosity toward Deputy **James A Weaver, Jr**, who'd conducted himself quite scrupulously despite that stupid arrest. I'd sensed he was one uptight, strung out, aging(albeit gentlemanly)cop. And I was likely close to being pretty correct.

Roughly just a decade later I spotted his obituary in the *Pensacola News–Journal.*

Cpl. James Arley Weaver, Jr—a 13–year veteran and investigator for the Escambia County Sheriff's Department—died of heart disease at a Pensacola hospital Friday afternoon the **16th of September 1983**. Born the **25th of July 1930** Weaver was just **53** years old.

RIP, *Slick!*

THREE:

PJC

POLICE

RECRUIT

TRAINING

"ACADEMY"

*"I think all psychiatrists and psychologists are basically **crazy**—as are most **policemen**."—**Jim Chancy***

I kept on the straight and narrow until August 1981 when at 27 I enrolled in the so–called *"Police Recruit Training"* academy program at *Pensacola Junior College(PJC)*, Class #37. On **11 June 1980** the previous summer I'd graduated from PJC with its lame–ass Associate of Science(AA) degree in Law Enforcement—a program I'd started right out of high school in 1972 but left unfinished. On **11 December 1981** the *Florida Commission on Criminal Justice Standards and Training* awarded me its **Certificate of Completion in Law Enforcement**— *"For having satisfactorily completed the police training program as established in Chapter 943.14(1), Florida Statutes **1981** as amended and in partial fulfillment of the requirements for employment as a police officer as required by law."* Its dutiful disclaimer: *"Not Valid For Employment."* Days later on **14 December 1981** PJC's School of Career Development, Department of Law Enforcement, certified that I successfully completed **Police Recruit Academy #37**. PJC's so–called "Institute of Criminal Justice," Department of Public Service Careers, likewise certified **14 December 1981** that I successfully completed **Police Recruit Academy #37** with the extra bonus of a **"#1 in Physical Training."**

I was especially proud of scoring an ending total of 407 points for a 100% grade—racking up 352 points for the mid–term test #1 and 396 points for the final test with 11 points added—for my physical training scores undertaken Monday the 23rd of November 1981.

In the allotted minute I completed 48 of my 50 push–ups and 100 sit–ups respectively and ran a 66–second quarter mile(just three seconds slower than the very first timed quarter mile I ran in high school); just a 90–second quarter was required for a 100% rating. Unfortunately I never recorded my time for our 12–minute run for which 1.7 miles rated 100%, which I clearly completed, finishing in excess of 1.5 miles.

It was a marked improvement over my first round of physical training tests undertaken Tuesday the 1st of September 1981 when I completed 46 push–ups and 60 sit–ups and ran my quarter mile in 74 seconds.

Sunday the 25th of October 1981 I ran(#303)together with several fellow police academy candidates Pensacola's first so–called *"Great American Bay Race"*—a 6.2–mile race of 515 runners across Pensacola Bay via its three–mile bay bridge, ending at the *Bahama Bay Club* in Gulf Breeze, Florida.

Today PJC's less grandiose–sounding *"Criminal Justice Technology Program"* is under its Behavioral Sciences Department.

So pleased and proud was I about my epic accomplishment that on the evening of PJC's police recruit academy #37 graduation ceremony I preferred staying home to watch on CBS TV(originally NBC)the annually repeated presentation of the *Arthur Rankin Jr–Jules Bass/Production* Christmas stop–motion animation family classic, **Rudolph The Red–Nosed Reindeer(1964)**—in consecutive years the longest–running Christmas TV special!

§

Attending PJC's **Police Recruit Training Academy #37** proved to be quite the proverbial insider eye–opening(if not eye–popping)experience, implicating typical impotent cop attitudes. Consider these excerpts quoted from actual "academy" instructors:

•*"If you're involved in a minor auto accident with property damage but no injuries—and you're already drunk—leave the scene, head for the nearest bar and drink in front of witnesses."*—**Don Grant**, **Levin Law Firm**, shyster attorney advising cops how to avoid driving under the influence(*DUI*), driving while intoxicated(*DWI*), drunk driving, drinking and driving, drunk–driving charges.

§

All the following self–explaining–and–revealing declarations were quoted from **Officer Chapman, Pensacola Police Department(PPD):**

•*"Get your charges from your narrative report—or they won't stick."*

•*"Anybody who commits these sexual batteries is* **sick**.*"*

•*"We just* **harassed** *the hell out of 'em(***"whores"***)."*

•*"Under the old jailhouse system the county judge told a potential informant: 'you either talk to the police or go to jail for 30 days.'"*

•*"Take a little lip or do two hours of paperwork. It depends on the situation and the circumstances, what they say, how it hurts, how I feel that day."*(the objective decision–making process for arresting citizens who **verbally** object to or protest against police actions)

•*"I don't have to take no* **bull–shit** *off nobody."*

•*"It has always intrigued me that there are two kinds of people: one kind on the street and another kind in court."*(two kinds of **cops** too no doubt)

•*"Liars will lie pacifically."*

•*"Attorneys like police to do all the work. Sometimes they have to do some work themselves."*

•*"The best* **survivors** *are the best* **liars**. *The best* **salesmen** *are the best* **liars**.*"*

•*"Take smart–ass or butt–showing suspects back to*

the tank."

•"I just jerk 'em("defensive" suspects)up and throw 'em back in the slammer. I tell 'em, 'I don't need to talk to you. I got you without a statement. I was just doin' you a favor by talkin' to you.'"

•"That's because I think a lot of these people—these experts who assert that **homosexuality** is an acceptable way of life—are **homosexuals** themselves."

•"Psychologists say **incest** is a one–time thing. That's **horse manure**. It's reported once but it goes on."

•"I didn't want these kids anywhere from seven to ten years old to get up in court to testify against this **son–of–a–bitch**(a child molester). And he is one too."

•"When you become a policeman you do what **society** don't want to do."

•"Being a police officer is a **disease**. Once you get it in your blood you can't get it out."

•"A **good shooting** of a suspect occurs when the guy **deserved** to be **shot**."

•"Many people have bought respectability with money and financial status. But to police they're **Joe–Blows** on the street."

•"Listen, **rubber jaws**."(Chapman's address to **"jawin'"** citizen bystanders or onlookers)

•"Knowin' me I believe in **aggressive** law enforcement, **aggressive** patrol and whatnot."

•"If you wanna be a hundred percent bona fide **prick** be one if necessary to settle things down"(in "domestic disturbance" calls)

•"Everything else in society set up to help people(churches, rehabilitation organizations)has failed and they expect the police to solve the problem."

•"Some people(men who try to regain the affections of estranged women)just don't realize there's more than *one woman in the world."*

•*"You gotta do what you gotta do when you gotta do it."*

•*"When I go I go **prepared to shoot**"*(chasing after "fleeing felons")

•*"People who start committin' these types of felonies*(murder, robbery, rape)*got no business bein' on the streets."*

•*"I'm goin' to do anything I can do to get 'em*(murderers, robbers, rapists)*off the street."*

•*"He's really perverted."*(**T Brewer,** a man in love with an 11–year–old girl who left his family and children)

•*"Threaten*(an uncooperative pawn shop dealer who's a **"snot"**)*to procure a search warrant, serve it at 3AM, and if something illegal is found promise the owner will spend two weeks daily in court before ever being called to testify. I learned that trick from the **FBI**."*(well, **Bravo!**)

•*"They ain't got any respect for a dead body at the **hospital**."*

•*"You can see these fruits*("kleptomaniacs"), *you know, these queers, and peg 'em right away."*

•*"Sexual deviants usually remain uncured."*

•*"It's a **game**(incest)the whole family can play."*

•*"She'd make a clock run backwards. Somebody beat her*(serial killer Ted Bundy's girlfriend)*with the **ugly stick**."*

•*"I thought that*(Miami hotel burglary)*was befitting somebody*(Ted Bundy's girlfriend)*who'd chase a guy*(Ted Bundy)*like that."*

•*"There are some things you just don't talk about."*

•*"The number one problem in any agency is first line supervision."*

•*"You don't have to take anything off anybody on*

the street if you know what you're doin'."

•"You can cause them(attorneys)a lot more embarrassment than they can cause you."

•"If there's a doubt always go with the higher charge."

*•"When it comes time to charge these people sometimes I **load their butt down** to keep them off the street."*

*•"I never lie to them(interview suspects). There are certain things I might **leave out** while I'm talking to them."*

§

All the following self–explaining–and–revealing declarations were quoted from **Roy Kinsey**, shyster **wattle–loving** Pensacola attorney:

•"Halfway houses don't do anybody a damn bit of good anyway."

•*"I felt guilty about defending that **turkey**."*(referring to **Willie Watts**, shooter of a convenience store victim)

• *"Officers shouldn't have to pay it."*(attorneys fees for cops involved in civil rights–related shooting incidents)

•*"The **turkey** didn't deserve them."*(referring to a defendant acquitted of a criminal charge receiving monetary damages for being physically abused by cops)

§

Sage bromides and trite platitudes from Mr. **Grant, Pensacola Police Department(PPD):**

•**"Ass/u/me** *nothing in police work or else you make an **ass** out of **you** and **me**."*

•*"The safest gun in the world is a loaded weapon*

out of a human being's hands."

•*"The second safest gun in the world is one with its hammer cocked but equipped with a fail safe mechanism."*

•*"I hate to say this: you cannot arrest or try him(a diplomat who's committed a felony). But you sure can stop him. You can prevent him from committing a felony—especially a crime against a person. That's as far as I'd like to comment in a public class."*(what's to hide?)

•*"There is no such charge as* **disrespect** *for a police officer."*

•*"Federal judges have taken powers they have no authority to take. I hope the Congress removes some of this authority."*

•*"You should treat violators as you'd like to be treated. But there are problems with that statement."*

•*"Police are notorious about* **breaking** *speeding laws."*

•*"It's not uncommon for this to happen. It's a big joke in police circles to carry a* **throw–down gun**(a *planted gun). But I've never seen it."*

§

All these declarations concerning courtroom testimony are quoted from Mr. **Kerrigan**, shyster attorney:

•*"Officers* **lie regularly under oath** *and* **have no ethical standards** *on the stand."*

•*"It's been my experience that* **lying** *is just commonplace in court."*

•*"Be careful about* **shading** *and* **exaggerating** *testimony."*

•*"Some officers feel someone's attitude must be exaggerated to be really understood."*

•*"There's so little humor in the courtroom it's* **sick**.*"*
•*"In cross examination the leading question is the greatest weapon in the arsenal of a lawyer."*
And Mr. **Rankin**, shyster attorney:
•*"Judges don't give a shit."*
•*"Eyewitness testimony is the easiest and most common way justice is subverted and innocent people get convicted—especially when an eyewitness actually believes a suggestion to the mind which is wrong."*

§

Sage saws quoted from **"Art" Scroggs**:
•*"It's easier to get forgiveness than prior approval."*

§

Criminal conduct–coaching quoted from Neanderthal instructor, **Al Winfield**:
•*"Child abuse is one thing I'd seriously* **kill** *for. I'd uphold my officers too. We might have to* **lie** *a lot."*
•*"I'm not telling you to* **kick the door down** *to do it(taking custody of an abused child). But I'm not telling you you can't either."*
•*"I'm very* **forceful** *in this area and* **cross the boundaries***(between legal and illegal action)sometimes. But I always* **cover my tail end** *when I do it."*
•*"You've got to be* **conservative** *to be a* **cop***, don't ya? If you're a* **liberal** *you're in* **trouble** *out there."*
•*"All the kids in the* **'60s deserved spankings***. If they had been* **disciplined** *as they should've been we wouldn't have had the* **'70s***."*
•*"Our criminal justice system back here leaves something to be desired. Prosecutors usually cop them down to a lower charge. So go with everything(by*

way of charges)you can."

•*"There's still a very unique thing out here in the South—and that's respect. It's sliding away on us but it's still out there."*

•*"There is respect for law enforcement here(in the South)even though they kill us more(than on the west coast). There's more respect for parents in the South."*

•*"**Reasoning with children**—a concept existing thanks to **Dr Spock**(renowned pediatrician, **Benjamin McLane Spock**)and the like—is **bullcrap**."*

•*"The **supreme law of the land** should come right out of the **Bible**."*

•*"What was the cause of the permissive raising of children? It was because of people like **Dr Spock**(renowned pediatrician, **Benjamin McLane Spock**)."*

•*"Police are expected to take up where the parents leave off."*

•*"I think every police department needs **Clint Eastwood(as "Dirty Harry")**. We need to keep him in a back room somewhere and take him out when we need him. But we couldn't give him too much exposure or we'd lose him."*

•*"All we're going to do is treat them("troubled" children)like criminals. Are we going to help them? No. Because of time constraints police just process them."*

§

Richard Day of the **Levin Law Firm**:

•*"It(DUI, DWI)will probably have more social implications than any other arrest. So sometimes it becomes very convenient to drop, reduce or otherwise convert the charge."*

•*"**Washing cars** is what **trustees** were invented for."*

•*"**Wrecker drivers** are notorious for **removing**(from vehicles)things of value."*

§

Jim Chancy:

•*"Don't we sometimes **fudge** our way through on our **authority**?"*

•*"If there's any doubt put your hands **anywhere** to protect yourself. **Damn the modesty.** Discreet searches are **bull–shit**."*

•*"You don't have to put it(a dismantled wrecker–impounded vehicle belonging to a suspect objecting to a trunk search)back together."*

§

Ron Roswell:

•*"I ain't got nothin' against long hair. I married a girl with long hair. It's just when I see it on a male that I have trouble."*

•*"Get there(a fight call)as long after the fight has started as possible. Because if you get in a fight they'll(the fighters)already be tired. And they may leave the scene before you arrive."*

•*"Psychologically it's a **coerced interrogation.** You got to get him before he gets his attorney. **I've violated the hell out of people's rights and probably will continue to do so.**"*(advocating lawyerless interviews with six uniformed cops, one with a wet towel, in a bare brightly–lit room with a slow–leaking water faucet)

§

Josey:

•*"Juries are too lenient especially when they **fall for** the(white collar crime)defendant's **sympathy act** over **hardship** cases."*

§

The upshot of all these sage and wise chestnuts: all police–arrested suspects simply *must* be guilty until proven innocent and merit summary police execution if it could be gotten away with!

FOUR:

BERKELEY'S

FINEST,

THE

UTTERLY

USELESS,

PENNY–

ANTE

POLICE

Serious violent crime occurs at a rampant rate in the frequently deadly corridor stretching the length of the close–knit towns bordering the San Francisco East Bay "flatlands," so–called, between Oakland and Richmond, California—two of the country's(and the state's)crime capitals specializing in endemic mostly black(64.7 homicide suspects)–on–black(77% homicide victims)murder over a five–year average; males made up 96% and 88% of the suspects and victims respectively.

Spanning a five–year period Oakland boasted 109, 88, 94, 145, 120 and 124 homicides per year for 2003–2008 respectively. In 2007 its homicidal sister city, Richmond, bested Oakland to take 2nd place behind Compton for recording California's top three highest murder rates.

Per capita in 2007 Oakland ranked twice the robbery and rape rates than Richmond and Compton.

Much of this violent crime literally bleeds over into Berkeley, which is sandwiched between these two crime capitals, and where Berkeley's Finest cope with it in their own exceptionally unique and specialized fashion: by going into hiding and seeking easy marks!

Over a period of residence spanning 13 years I've personally observed and witnessed countless episodes of the innocuous "criminal" elements—both equally harmless and defenseless—most targeted by the Berkeley *Bog*'s most impotent law enforcement personnel: the homeless and *Cal* university students!

I've personally experienced as well how these impotent shirkers deliberately dodge their more important and primary duties.

§

Friday the 4th of January 1991 the United Nations Security Council spent its time condemning Israel's treatment of the Palestinians. At least the UN Security Council had its priorities straight!

Early that very same Friday evening at about 6:30PM I was bowling along south on Shattuck Avenue—on a ten–speed bicycle—headed for an imminent right turn at my upcoming cross street, Haste.

At Durant Avenue, another nearby cross street, an impotent Berkeley *Bog* cop driving a cruiser car actually flashed me with his lights, pulling me over to stop in front of the Berkeley *Bog*'s premier pseudo–Italian restaurant, *Giovanni's Pizza*, at 2420 Shattuck Avenue.

He accused me of "running a red light" and actually issued me a non–fine citation(#**9202686 9**)for having no "bike light."

"I'll give you a break," said the impotent gent—by issuing the non–fine citation and leaving off my driver's license number(well, he had to leave it off as I had no driver's license on my person to display!). Most magnanimous of him all the same!

But I was still obligated to obtain a so–called *"Certificate of Correction"* for the lack of the "bike light." So by the 28th of that very same month—since it cost me nothing—I showed my duly installed "bike light" to another impotent cop, doing nothing in particular in the "downtown" Berkeley *Bog*, and solicited him to kindly certify the "correction" by ticking it off with his dated signature!

My dear readers, this is serious and critical crime–busting not to mention pressing(and impressive impotent)priority police work!

§

The western boundary of *Tilden Regional Park* in San Francisco's East Bay follows the crest of the Berkeley Hills, threading the entire length of the Berkeley *Bog* and defining the town's easternmost elevated limit. *Grizzly Peak Boulevard* follows the winding ridgeline of the Berkeley Hills connecting to *Skyline Boulevard*, which stretches to the so–called Oakland Hills—technically the extension of the Berkeley Hills. Situated at intervals along the way are multiple spacious dirt–and–gravel turnouts with panoramic vistas overlooking San Francisco Bay and its magnificent cityscape beyond from on high. Those lofty spots are perfect for parking and taking in the breathtaking, awe–inspiring views— and fucking breathlessly whilst doing it! They likewise make popular and well–populated lovers' lanes.

So impotent, voyeuristic, pervert cops incapable of getting any themselves are quite naturally out *in force* to screw up the frolicsome good times of anybody and everybody capable of hotly screwing they can pervertedly peep at and interrupt in mid–copulation! These aren't the crime–busters but rather the intrepid but impotent armed–and–uniformed *SEX*–busters!

The very night before Lorena cut off John Wayne Bobbitt's penis on Tuesday the 22nd of June 1993 I was forcefully pumping mine into the sirupy pussy of my ready, willing and comely young Korean–American mistress in the passenger seat of her car parked at *Tilden Park*'s vista point looking out on San Francisco Bay.

Out of the blue in the dark dead of night a big cobalt metallic tank of an unmarked prowl car suddenly(and recklessly)swerved off the winding ridgeline road, and came barreling right up to an abrupt stop at her car's passenger side—blinding headlights blazing! Next the impotent cop driving the tank rudely threw his spotlight on us. Next the impotent cop got out of his tank to shine us with his dinky–dick, hand–held flashlight.

Most mistakenly thinking that both implements enlarge their phallus size impotent cops incapable of getting any of their own are powerfully queer for their sex–toy nightsticks and flashlights!

This cowboy with the Wyatt Earp moustache most mistakenly thought he'd terrorized us with all that radiant irradiation. He was dead wrong. I didn't budge or flinch an inch, keeping her completely covered with myself. She shut her eyes and slumped into silent slumber.

"What's the problem here?" I thought I heard him ask but was unsure even though *he himself* was the "problem" if one existed at all.

"What?" I ask, conspicuously perturbed.

"Pardon me?" he says dumbly.

"Is that necessary?" I snap.

"How old are you?"

"Thirty-nine!" I reply emphatically.

"How old is she?"

"Twenty-seven!" equally emphatic.

Facing us I staringly watched him ashamedly avert his eyes from us.

Without a word of warning or rebuke the impotent pervert cop ultimately turned on his heel, got back in his great big revved up tank and drove off.

Once he left we fully *finished* fucking at our leisure!

My dear readers, this is serious and solemn sex–busting not to mention pressing(and impressive impotent)priority police work!

§

Saturday the 25th of September 1993 my comely

48

Korean–American mistress and myself underwent an uncanny double–whammy of incredibly impotent police work!

Earlier in the evening she drove us to the *Wells Fargo Bank* in the Berkeley *Bog* at 2144 Shattuck Avenue so that she could stop to deposit checks and withdraw some cash from the bank's automated teller machine(ATM)dispenser.

Hastily she parked her idling car at the corner cross street(Center)at the westward foot of the bus stop's elongated red zone curb. Her car rested almost exactly half in and half out of the distant end of that red curb— barely infringing upon the prohibited parking space.

Before long an impotent *Alameda County Sheriff's Office(ACSO)* deputy—technically way out of his patrol and investigative jurisdiction—was rapping at the driver's window.

"Where's the driver?" he asked.

"At the bank," I answered.

"Is the driver a friend of yours?"

"Yes, of course she is."

Just then she returned to take her seat behind the wheel.

"You're parked halfway in a red zone," the impotent cop accused her, announcing the blatantly obvious. "Give me a good reason why I shouldn't give you a $270–plus ticket for illegally parking here, which is against California law."

Struck speechless she stayed silent.

"Oh," I groaned, breaking the overlong silence and putting on quite an act on her behalf, deliberately and innocently looking down at the curb through the passenger window and pausing for effect before replying.

"Because we're really not blocking any buses...and because you're a nice guy!" I carefully volunteered.

Struck dumb himself the impotent cop ignored me but scolded her.

"I'll give you a free warning instead of a costly parking ticket," he condescended magnanimously.

These preachy impotent bastards habitually abuse their cop parking privileges to idle their prowl cars in those very same bus stop red zones to make those very same transient cash–taking visits to bank ATMs—I've observed and witnessed their transgressions countless times!

It's a classic case of: do as I say, not as I monkey–do! In any case trolling bus stop red zones for parking violators is most definitely not amongst the *ACSO*'s primary responsibilities.

My dear readers, this is serious and solemn crime–busting not to mention pressing(and impressive impotent)priority police work!

§

Later on that very same Saturday night the 25th of September 1993 following dinner at *Plearn Thai Restaurant*, 1923 University Avenue, we drove back together to the "downtown" Berkeley *Bog*, parking quite legally to simply talk off Shattuck Avenue at a quiet side street—Berkeley Way—in(get *THIS!*)—a freakin' ***METERED PARKING SPACE!***

There we got accosted by the two equally impotent black boy–and–girl rookie cop partners from hell!

Out of the blue these jerk–offs first flashed us of course with their prowl car's spotlight—standard operating procedure for impotent cops so queer for their bright–light implements!

"Are we bothering someone?" I asked ironically the impotent black boy cop shining us with his dinky–dick, hand—held flashlight, rapping on the driver's window.

"Because you both were *slumped over* in the front seat" was the impotent black boy cop's pretext for accosting us—not exactly defensible probable cause for any reasonable suspicion.

In actual fact we were simply sitting embraced, arm—in—arm, our heads resting together—not *"slumped"*—whilst we were talking.

Next the impotent black boy cop demands our IDs.

"See why I want to move from here?" I ask her.

Coming back to return our IDs the impotent black boy cop was accompanied by his impotent black girl cop, rudely rapping—banging actually—on the passenger window.

"Is that necessary?" I ask testily. "What is it?"

"What's that on the floor there?" the impotent bitch asks dumbly.

"A bottle of apple juice," I reply, holding up the criminal contraband in front of her stupid face before dumping it back onto the floorboard. "Do you want to search the car next?"

"Are you giving me consent to search her car?" the impotent bitch asks even more dumbly.

Now I just love it when idiots try to get pseudo—intellectual with me!

"It's not my consent to give, is it?" I retort, stopping her bull—shit dead in its tracks.

She returned no reply.

"Look," I turn to the other impotent boy cop. "May we go now?"

"Yes," the impotent voyeuristic black boy cop conceded. "I'd suggest you find someplace else to sit, *smooch* and talk—because when I came up you had your hand on her breast."

He never saw us "smooch" because we hadn't committed that atrocious act the entire time we'd been sitting there.

In actual fact my right palm rested modestly above her left tanktop–covered breast—as if it were any of his fucking business where I placed my palms on my girlfriend's person with her willing consent in a car legally parked in a metered parking space!

"It was resting there. I wasn't groping her. And we weren't making out," I corrected him. "So we'll be off. Let's go."

"And you know," I added whilst she was rolling up her driver's window, "I really wish you'd do something about the armed robbers in this town while you're at it."

The impotent black boy cop mumbled something in reply but the sealed window muffled it.

§

Ah *ha!* Monday the 22nd of August 1994 I was passing by the front of *Blockbuster* at 2352 Shattuck Avenue in the Berkeley *Bog* where I happened upon this familiar obnoxious black clod "meter maid"—oh, ex–*cuse* me!—*"Parking Enforcement Officer(PEO),"* madly punching the keys of his portable keyboard with the license tag number of a car parked at a curb space meter displaying that foreboding red "Time Expired" flag!

Obnoxious, I say, because he had this psychotic penchant for impudently reprimanding and scolding car owners—females in particular—returning to cars parked at expired meters in his presence!

Promptly I stepped up to insert a couple nickels into that expired meter.

"I got you, sir!" he gloated out aloud.

I grinned widely, shaking my head.

"That's just to spite *you!*" I gloated right back. "This

isn't my car!"

"There are a couple more(cars parked at expired meters)down there," he challenged me, gesturing to the proximate row of metered curb spaces. "Why don't you put coins in those too?"

Good idea, happy to oblige!

Hurriedly I pressed nickels or dimes into two more expired meters. Passing by I overheard him calling in my physical description to his dispatcher by radio.

"You ain't got *me*, brother!" I blustered in passing. "You're a *joke!*"

As a prudent precaution though I slipped into a nearby photocopy shop(the now defunct *Copy Perfect*) I patronized, changed into a sweat suit to disguise my reported description, exited the shop through its open back door and returned to confidently stride the avenue again by way of the adjoining side street—adroitly removing any pretext for being accosted by some impotent cop out to harass some easy mark!

I *knew* my regular stamping ground!

§

Unless you're a landed member of the aristocratic gentry there's no "free" parking anyplace on the streets of the Berkeley *Bog* except at metered parking spaces between roughly sunset and sunrise—and even then just on certain sides of the street on certain days of the week whilst the supposedly "progressive" city resorts to "street cleaning"(its streets must rate as some of the smuttiest on the planet!)as a pretext for issuing costly parking tickets. Even on so–called "residential" neighborhood streets there's no "free" parking for apartment residents without paid annual parking permits. Even for visitors to those very same "residential" neighbor-

hoods there's just two–hour parking before roving meter maids chalk your tires and issue tickets based little
more on guesswork so far as parking expiration goes!

For my comely Korean–American mistress, resid-
ing at a ramshackle apartment building at 1915–1/2
Addison Street #101—a narrow east–west side street between the main drags running north–south—Shattuck
Avenue and Martin Luther King Jr Way(old Grove
Street), there was no overnight "residential" parking at
all without getting up at the crack of dawn each and every morning to move your car from some metered parking space to a nearby "neighborhood" street curb—for
which she was compelled to purchase an annual "residential" parking permit for a neighborhood she didn't
even live in!

So as a practical matter she had to temporarily visit
her own so–called "downtown" apartment and move
her car to park literally blocks away at a curb in the
nearby "neighborhood" where she didn't even live—for
which privilege she had to purchase an annual "residential" parking permit!

So late that night well past midnight in the wee early
hours of Saturday morning the 15th of July 1995 I was
doing her the favor of moving her car by driving it from
her "downtown" apartment to park it at a "residential"
curb in the nearby "neighborhood," which happened to
be quite close to the Berkeley *Bog* police department
building located today at 2100 Martin Luther King Jr
Way(old Grove Street).

So in the process of re–parking her car that night I
drove just a short haul west on Addison Street, passing
by the corner stop sign to cross over old Grove Street—a
fairly narrow four–lane road running north–south—
headed for the "residential neighborhood" in the imme-
diate vicinity of the Berkeley *Bog* police station itself.

It was right around two o'clock in the freakin' morning and there literally wasn't another motor vehicle in sight in the dead of night—in any direction. I came to a complete stop at the intersection and made a perfectly safe and excruciatingly slow crossing of Old Grove Street. The only trouble was: crossing there was technically prohibited as there was a posted restricted right turn–only at that Addison Street stop sign.

Once across old Grove Street I made another perfectly safe and excruciatingly slow U–turn on that side of the crosswise Addison Street to park her car at a "residential neighborhood" curb space bordering the north end of the Berkeley *Bog* police station building—even left–signaling my U–turn to all those non–existent motor vehicles not in sight!

Abruptly—and melodramatically—an impotent Berkeley *Bog* cop barreled right up in his prowl car at breakneck speed, cutting me off before I could parallel park by actually crossing over the middle of that narrow side street into my path and aiming the front of his car directly—and dangerously—at the front of mine.

In his "hot pursuit" of my overly–cautious snail–paced parking maneuver this particular impotent cop broke multiple traffic "laws" simply to overtake me to prove that Big Brother was watching—and to deliver to me a midnight lecture about the "law." It was almost too absurd for words!

First he sped dangerously and recklessly through a residential neighborhood. Next he sped through the stop sign and violated the very same posted restricted right turn–only at that intersection to catch up with me. Then he crossed the road median, violating my forward–moving right–of–way with a near head–on collision! This impotent jerk–off cop was friggin' *NUTS!* His name was **Montez**.

At first he flashed his prowl car's roof lights at me just momentarily. Finally he accosted me through his driver's window, staying seated behind his steering wheel.

"How long have you lived in the neighborhood?" he asks.

"A couple of months," I lied. By that time I'd already lived in the Berkeley *Bog* some *nine* long years—though not in that particular "neighborhood."

"Did you see the right turn–only sign and arrow you crossed?" he asks.

"Yes," I readily admitted, asking in turn. "At *this* hour?"

"There's a reason for the traffic signs and arrows," he lectures. "To prevent accidents. How do you justify ignoring them?"

"There's a spirit and a substance of a thing," I readily replied—as in the letter versus the spirit of the law. "There was no traffic to have accidents with."

"Let's do it this way then," he says, getting grandly out of his car, getting my car's license number, taking my driver's license and writing me a traffic ticket—the exceptional specialty of impotent Berkeley *Bog* cops.

"How would you rationalize breaking the law to a judge?" he asks me, dragging out this powerfully stupid conversation even further.

"I made a perfectly safe crossing with no traffic in sight in either direction!" I retorted without hesitation.

Anything else? Naturally there was.

"I'm citing you under a city ordinance for disobeying a traffic device that won't appear on your driving record," he informed me.

"I'll appeal it, no problem," I said wearily.

"Just remember our discussion," he admonishes me, handing me the ticket.

"What am I supposed to remember about it?" I ask.

"I don't know what else to tell you, Mr. Covino," he lectures further, "but you can't break the law when you decide it's all right to do so, or when you think no one else is around—because someone else *is* around!"

Yes indeed, Big Brother's always watching—except of course when he could possibly be of any substantial assistance to anybody.

"What I'll remember," I told him point–blank, "is that you guys are nowhere to be found when something important is happening, and that when something important *is* happening, you guys go into hiding!"

"Do you want to vent anything more?" he asks me, turning his hand with a cranking motion.

"Not at all," I retorted—as if there'd be any point he could conceivably comprehend. "I'm just trying to park. May I go now?"

"Sure."

"Thank you."

As I was finally backing her eastward–facing car into my targeted parking space this preachy impotent cop abruptly braked and sped recklessly around and past me—*again!*—after making the very same U–turn I'd done earlier!

Utterly unbelievable!

To date I haven't owned a motor vehicle in California since April 1987—especially since an automobile is for that particular oppressive police state nothing but a deliberate tool of legalized extortion. So as a rule—since I own no car to be extorted with—I outright refuse to pander to impotent cop egos by paying traffic tickets issued me whilst driving other people's cars.

This case was no different:

At the outset that ticket's extortion(**338392X**)supposedly cost $75! By 25 October 1995 that *unpaid* ticket's extortion had increased to the exorbitant amount of $217!

I expressly own no car to be towed to coerce extortion or to be confiscated and auctioned off by impotent cops.

It *remained* **un**paid until it finally went off my driving record permanently!

§

Now this was *really* **WEIRD!**

Late Tuesday night the 13th of February 1996 I'd just left the *Edwards Stadium/Goldman Field* track & field facility at the foot of *Cal* campus in the Berkeley *Bog* after running, stretching and vocalizing to exercise my singing voice.

I was footing it north along the four–lane, north–south Fulton/Oxford Streets drag, heading for my comely Korean–American mistress' nearby apartment to visit, singing softly en route.

Some impotent Berkeley *Bog* cop abruptly passed me by in his prowl car, sped up to the upcoming four–lane, east–west cross street—University Avenue—screeching and swerving whilst making a reckless U–turn at the red light, speeding back towards me. I'd just turned off left to stride westward along the preceding two–way, east–west cross street of Addison.

As I was crossing Fulton/Oxford Streets the impotent Berkeley *Bog* cop abruptly pulled up, stopping just short of the intersection to idle his prowl car and glare indignantly at me through his open driver's window.

"Yes?" I asked, staring back suspiciously at him as I calmly crossed the street in front of his prowl car.

He drove off behind me as abruptly as he'd drove up. *100%* **WEIRD!**

§

Late Wednesday night the 6th of November 1996 my new–found buxom young Brazilian babe, Tina, whom I'd recently met at the "downtown" Berkeley *Bog* YMCA's hot tub, decided quite spontaneously that she wanted to take me "someplace nice" where I'd never been or seen before. So she volunteered to drive us to *Indian Rock Park*, a 1.18–acre public park situated on the slope of the Berkeley Bog Hills in the northeast part of town, straddling Indian Rock Avenue about one block north of the Arlington/Marin Circle. The park's central feature is a considerable volcanic rock outcropping—topped by *Indian Rock* itself—on Indian Rock Ave's westward side.

Supposedly this **crock o' Rock** commands "spectacular" views of the surrounding San Francisco Bay, but naturally at that time of night(near midnight)it's too dark out to make out the rock itself much less the encompassing environs.

Parked at a neighborhood curb we got out of Tina's car and started to tread a path into the park.

No sooner had we bent our steps toward that park did the omnipresent, omni(m)potent Berkeley *Bog* cop skulk by in his silently coasting prowl car, ordering us through his open window to read the sign posting the park's hours and closing time(10PM), which had already expired.

We can only speculate about how long that shiftless shirker/slacker of an impotent Berkeley *Bog* crime–buster must've been lying in wait there before exposing himself simply to screw up some amorous couple's chances of getting some action.

Keeping the Berkeley *Bog safe for celibacy* is a peculiar specialty of the impotent Berkeley *Bog* cop!

§

Friday afternoon in the Berkeley *Bog* I came across a past acquaintance of mine named Cassie sitting atop the brick hedge outside the main "downtown" *Bank of America* branch at 2129 Shattuck Avenue. Cassie was the sexy black manager of the nearby transient *Cal Hotel* at 2008 Shattuck Avenue where she once rented me a room for roughly a week during August 1988.

A pair of impotent male–and–female Berkeley *Bog* cops awaited admittance through the westward doors of the bank, evidently closed early due to some police episode.

"I feel so safe and protected with them here," Cassie cracked.

"You must be kidding!" I exclaimed aloud. "I feel more endangered being around people with guns who don't know how to use them!"

As I was marching off the pair of impotent cops followed right behind me, heading for the bank's opposite southward doors.

"Oh, that's very funny," cracked the insulted impotent dyke–like cop, overhearing me. "You're a real comedian!"

I wasn't trying to be funny—I was deadly serious!

"Yeah, that's right," I readily agreed, "and I'm entitled to my opinion because it's still a free country since the fascists haven't yet taken over—though I know you're trying!"

No clever rejoinder from those two impotent Berkeley *Bog* cops to *that!*

§

Sunday the 13th of February 2000 was the last time

the original syndicated "Charlie Brown" *Peanuts* comic strip was published following the death the day before of its creator, *Charles M Schulz*, of complications from colon cancer in Santa Rosa, seat of Sonoma County in California's wine country.

Early that evening in the Berkeley *Bog* I was driving along with my voluptuous Filipina–American mistress in her mother's car. We'd just left a metered parking space on nearby University Avenue. I was steering south on Shattuck Avenue, rounding the corner at the very next block with a right turn onto the side street, Addison, cautiously driving excruciatingly slow.

It was growing dark and raining lightly outside; and I'd unknowingly turned the car's headlights knob only halfway to its "on" position just moments after pulling away from the curb we'd been parked at earlier. And of course impotent cops are absolutely perfect and never commit human mistakes.

Approaching us from the facing direction on Addison Street was an impotent cop, coasting his cruiser car slowly towards us, scowling grotesquely and inexplicably wagging his finger at us without a word—as if we were supposed to divine some psychic message from his deliberately rude gestures.

"*What?*" I frowned, rolling down my window in passing.

"Turn your lights on—*that's* what!" he snapped back, following that up with the typical impotent cop threat, "or else I'll give you a ticket!"

"Go ahead," I goaded him, "if that'll make your day."

So quite predictably he pulled us over and put us through that tedious and tiresome ID–check rigmarole, but reducing my girlfriend to tears since she couldn't readily find the vehicle's registration and insurance forms in its glove compartment.

Only after finding nothing in my squeaky–clean record that he could abuse his authority to arrest me for—out of sheer spite and pettiness—did he finally cite me, writing his ticket.

"You're being ugly in a no–ugly zone," he cracked crassly—after *he'd* been the one coming on with the ugly grimace and the vulgar gestures from the very beginning! Citizens, you see, are just supposed to take all that crap from impotent cops and never dare respond in kind. Well, not *this* citizen—not *ever!*

"Follow the rules of the road," he admonished me condescendingly afterwards.

He'd also attempted but failed to persuade my emotionally distraught girlfriend to drive the car instead of me since she was more "closely related to" the car's actual owner, her mother, and because he doubted my ability to operate the vehicle properly.

What a laugh! She not only let me resume driving her mother's car but actually fucked me forcefully in its front seat that very same night! So much for the persuasion powers of impotent cops!

This is the classic case of an impotent cop incapable of coping with any citizen challenge to his exiguous ego! Ugly in a no–ugly zone? This particular impotent cop was utterly useless in a be–useful zone—par for the course for the utterly useless, penny–ante impotent cops of the Berkeley *Bog*. Follow the rules of the road? This particular impotent cop sorely needs to learn how to follow the rules of humanity: common courtesy and human decency!

For these types of impotent cops petty spite is their sole over–riding rule of the road. Forget all about performing any pressing priority police work!

I'd dare this cowardly crime–buster(**Salas** by name)to publish his felony arrest record versus his traffic ticket citation record any day of the week!

At first the fine for this traffic ticket extortion(***Docket #: 918–841–7***)—for the trumped up cited violation of "lighting during dark"—amounted to $77! By 21 March 2002 the *unpaid* ticket's extortion had increased to $229!

As I expressly own no car to be towed to coerce extortion or to be confiscated to be auctioned off by impotent cops this ticket's extortion *remained **unpaid*** until it finally went off my driving record permanently—despite the California DMV's suspension of my "driving privileges" by 9 August 2000 and a "DMV Hold" being placed on my driver's license by 31 May 2004.

By 13 October 2005 I'd renewed my California driver's license even though I still resort to it only sparingly.

I defiantly and outright *REFUSE* ever to pay(or post)"bail"(or extortion)for trumped up traffic tickets simply to pander to the exiguous egos of impotent cops!

§

Today the Berkeley *Bog* police department's located at 2100 Martin Luther King Jr Way though in times past its main entrance opened out westward a block over onto McKinley Avenue. For a time I suffered the grievous misfortune of living directly across the street at 2124 McKinley Avenue in an apartment located in the rear of what its imperial "owner," Sigmund S Cohn, imperiously referred ever so formidably to as the "***BUILDING.***"

Saturday the 10th of October 1998 a familiar friend and fellow member of the so–called "downtown" Berkeley *Bog* YMCA drove me and my several bags home to the "***BUILDING***"(since I didn't drive)from the pretty distant "northside" *Safeway Food&Drug*,

at 1444 Shattuck Avenue, where we bumped into each other shopping.

My kindly friend, doing me this good turn, briefly idled his car double–parked in front of the entry to the "**BUILDING**," dropping off me and my goods.

Before long some impotent Asian Berkeley *Bog* cop pulled up to park in a slanted space his prowl car, flashing my friend with that bright, blinding spotlight all impotent cops are invariably so queer for, grumbling all the while.

"You're almost blocking my way into my space!" the impotent cop reprimanded my friend. "You've turned your lights off too!"

Folks, this is *GUT*–busting, *CRIME*–busting— a petty episode epitomizing perfectly why I dub the Berkeley *Bog* cops the *UTTERLY USELESS PENNY ANTE POLICE!*

§

Wednesday the 21st of October 1998—just several days later—I was just about to cross on foot Center Street at Shattuck Avenue in the so–called "downtown" Berkeley *Bog* slightly ahead of the changing green light traffic signal.

"Wait for the light!" this creep of an impotent Berkeley *Bog* cycle cop yells commandingly at me at the top of his voice from across the friggin' street.

"Yes sir!" I shouted back, bowing in front of God and dumbfounded bystanders, saluting him sarcastically with the Arabic breast–lips–forehead gesture of obeisance!

"Yeah!" was this impotent creep cycle cop's sole quick and clever comeback!

Folks, this is *GUT*–busting, *CRIME*–busting—another petty episode epitomizing perfectly why I dub the Berkeley *Bog* cops the *UTTERLY USELESS PENNY ANTE POLICE!*

§

Wednesday night the 30th of August 2000 I went to the movies in the Berkeley *Bog* with my comely Filipina–American mistress, whom I was driving home to distant San Leandro afterwards in her car. Discreetly bowling north–south along Martin Luther King Jr Way(Old Grove Street), speedily bound for the oncoming cross street of Ashby Avenue, I got promptly *NAILED* by a speed–trap cop parked in hiding on an eastward side cross street—whom I spotted but too late!

Presently we were pulled over and stopped by an elderly, portly and exceptionally unkempt but mellow black gentleman cop. I promptly put on the car's interior lights and gripped the steering wheel with both hands in full view.

"You must be in a *real* hurry," he suggested.

"No," I said nonchalantly, "not really."

"Do you know what the speed limit here is?"

"No."

"You don't?"

"Twenty-five miles per hour," I quickly corrected myself, "I should imagine."

"You were going fifty," he alleged.

"*Fifty?!*" I exclaimed, sounding innocently aghast.

"Well, approaching it," he hedged.

"I honestly hadn't noticed," I lied.

"Slow it down then," he advised, nodding.

"Yes sir," I assented, "I was just driving my girlfriend to the BART station."

"Take your foot off the gas pedal to avoid getting a

ticket that'll raise your insurance rates," he advised further.

"Thank you," I acquiesced again. "I promise I'll be careful."

I was taken aback by that black gentleman cop's easygoing, laid–back, patient and polite approach to the stop—in 46 years of living the pleasantest cop encounter for a speeding infraction I'd ever experienced anyplace.

He hadn't even subjected us to that extremely tedious and tiresome driver's license–insurance–and–registration rigmarole!

By this time I trust that he's enjoying a happy, peaceful and well–earned–and–deserved retirement someplace.

Lesson being: if you're courteous and polite to me then I'm more inclined to comport myself in a similar manner.

FIVE:

UC BERKELEY KEYSTONE COPS

Excerpted from my book, *Sexcapades by the Decades: The Thirties(2008)*:

At the *Waldenbooks* store Friday the 5th of January 1990 a fresh, extremely exotic, dark–complexioned acquaintance of mine named Hari(yes, as in Hare Krishna)handed me her telephone number. She was an ambitious and seemly go–getter who constantly acted as if she were a going concern. She claimed she kept a house in both nearby Richmond, California as well as an apartment in San Francisco since she was employed at the University of California at Berkeley and studied as a student at the University of California at San Francisco.

"School keeps me out of trouble," she confided, "meaning men since they're too demanding of my time."

Personally I'd be barely temporarily but quite pleasurably demanding of her time.

Roughly a week later the 15th of January 1990 Hari dropped by the bookstore to invite me out for a break at a nearby cafe on Center Street where she took an espresso and treated me to a hot tea. After my work-shift she showed up that night to pick me up in her car.

First Hari drove us to the *Cal* Facilities Management Office, located inside what used to be a residential house, which is purportedly responsible for the buildings, infrastructure and grounds of the UC Berkeley campus. At her desk there she worked briefly on a computer word processor to correct some typesetting to a report paper titled, *Attack of the Killer TVs*.

In the meantime she disclosed more about herself: she was originally from New York but had lived in the Berkeley *Bog* for the past six years. Her mother was South Indian, her father Greek, though she evaded revealing what he did for a living. She let on she was a spoilt brat, attending both the University of California and the University of San Francisco in the city. "They throw money at me for school," she admitted. She'd run the gamut of changing academic majors from business, engineering and psychotherapy. Surprisingly she was amongst that scant political minority who thought that the so–called *People's Park* in the Berkeley *Bog* should be closed down!

Next it was on to the popular and over–hyped student *Milano Cafe* at 2522 Bancroft Way where she treated me to a hot chocolate and we talked together for quite a long time.

"Black, foreign and other minority men date white blond women as status symbols," she griped at some point.

Fortunately that wasn't one of my fixations—far from it!

Finally Hari drove us up to the *The Ernest Orlando Lawrence Berkeley National Laboratory(LBNL)*—a U.S. Department of Energy(DOE)national laboratory supposedly conducting unclassified scientific research—to take in the distant but limited night–time panoramic view of San Francisco Bay. It's situated on 200 acres of *Cal's* grounds atop the Berkeley Hills, overlooking the central campus from high up above. It reputedly holds the distinction of being the oldest of the DOE's National Laboratories.

Before long some lumbering, overgrown, overbearing, mustached *Cal* campus cop skulked into the parking lot in his creeping cruiser car, spot–lighting parked cars, parking and emerging himself to make the rounds of all the parked cars in the lot, shining occupants with his flashlight.

Naturally the cop came up to accost us, our windows rolled down, ordering us imperiously to leave since the signpost closing time for the parking lot was nine–thirty at night. Before ever waddling off he lingered, shining his flashlight into the backseat of Hari's car.

"Do you see anything interesting back there?" I asked him quite simply.

"What did you say?" he asked challengingly, waddling back.

I repeated the excruciatingly simple question any simple–minded simpleton could readily comprehend.

He demanded to look at my ID and launched immediately into the typical impotent cop's habitually condescending lecture:

"I have to do a job because we have problems up here with violence, drugs and alcohol."

Whoa! The courageous and crusading crime–buster's Big 3 most perilous parking lot offenses!

"Do we look violent or do you see any drugs or alcohol?" I calmly questioned him further.

"I don't know you!" he snapped, planting his two fat flat feet and clasping his hands in front of himself, standing squarely in front of the passenger window. If ever there were an easy—not to mention a mightily stupid—target for an armed criminal car passenger!

Good God, who the fuck would want to know him?!

"Are you trying to impress me?" he rambled on. "You're not impressing me. Or are you trying to impress your friend?"

"Nobody's trying to impress you."

How could anybody impress a buffoonish, blockheaded neanderthal having such an extremely limited and primitive mentality?

"Look," I added, "you told us to leave and we're ready to go. So we'll be on our way if you don't mind."

"I do mind," he huffed, demanding to inspect Hari's vehicle registration.

Hari raised a hand to object.

"Just let him go through the motions," I said nonchalantly.

"Why are you checking my registration?" Hari asked him anyway.

"Because your friend has an attitude problem," he huffed.

So—naturally it's the courageous and crusading crime—buster's prime mission in life to teach tough lessons to innocuous citizens having attitude problems.

"Is there some law against asking you a question?" I pressed him further.

"You're being sarcastic," he huffed.

Oh my, book me then on a charge of criminal sarcasm!

Since he could trump up no petty charges to either ticket or arrest us for this blockheaded clod of a cop finally gave it up and gave us his magnanimous leave to go.

So go we did—with Hari driving us to park and talk at the curb on old Grove Street right around the corner from my nearby Haste Street flat.

"I liked the way you talked to that cop," Hari complimented me.

"I thought you were such a good—looking man," she confided, "and had an interesting face—and a lot of class in the way you carried yourself—but that I should leave you alone. But I noticed that you paid special attention to me at the bookstore; so that's why I talked to you."

I'd invited her in to visit upstairs.

"Maybe another time," she demurred.

Before long though we both expressed having need of the rest room.

"I'm not going to pass this up!" Hari finally consented once I invited her upstairs again.

"I feel very comfortable here," Hari said, plunking herself down right onto my twin–sized mattress after first briefly looking round my little flat.

"You'll be gentle with me with those?" I joked half–heartedly, clasping her hands warmly in mine to inspect the long, colored, sharp–looking, Fu Manchu–like nails, curling from her slender fingertips.

And she would be—heatedly, sweetly and intensely gentle!

"You have a very nice well–shaped body," she complimented me afterwards. "And you make very good love."

"I knew something would happen," she confessed. "I'll tell you later something I wrote down about it before. I'm deeply into the *meta*physical."

Afterwards I walked her outside to her car to see her off wearing my night robe.

When it came to pointedly penetrating Hari's pouring pussy that night I'd been deeply—and rapturously—into the *physical.* And it wouldn't be the first nor the last time some stupid, blockheaded clod of a cop would help me get laid but good!

§

The *Col. George C. Edwards Stadium/Goldman in–Field* on *Cal* campus is an exclusive but once open–door track & field facility where I used to run regularly at all hours of the day or night before so–called renovations—finished by 2000—restricted access/entry, making it an exclusionary track & field facility.

Every time a fresh top polyurethane all–weather track surface is laid, you see, community exclusion is typically the result.

In January 1995 the stadium's elevated access/entry

points at its frontward(northward)tennis courts were undergoing construction—chiefly the erection of this lofty and supposedly insurmountable bar–metal fence–gate adjoining the heavy and equally lofty green lumber service road gate coupled regularly with heavy–duty chain and padlock.

What the intellectual geniuses who fabricated this supposedly impenetrable barricade to free and open track access/entry wasn't the loftiness, but rather the *lowness* of their tall and slick metallic fence—for at a cement cornerstone at its foot, adjoining the side road pedestrian sidewalk, was left an admittedly extremely snug crawl–space underneath which, deflating your chest and ribcage sufficiently, you could slide supine right beneath the unyielding metal base beam. That's how I'd gain access/entry for nighttime running count-less times thereafter once all gates were locked and supposedly secured.

Thursday the 12th of January 1995 I found the chain–link construction fence actually rolled back, making for easy access/entry through an open gap that particular night.

Locked inside behind the adjoining tall green lum-ber service road gate though I discovered two idled cars and their gentleman drivers, who'd already called for help from the emergency blue–light campus cop phone located on the side of the tennis courts blockhouse at the foot of the sloping access road, which descends to the stadium field itself. By the time those two blokes were released from their involuntary captivity and let out with their vehicles I'd finished rounding the last couple of laps to my regular three–mile run.

On my own way out of the track & field on foot by way of that very same sloping service road I happened upon the prowl car of an impotent *Cal* campus cop, idling just beyond the tall green lumber service road gate—by then already chained and padlocked. So I figured he'd stopped simply to make doubly sure the gate was duly locked.

Wrong! This impotent *Cal* campus cop actually got out of his idling prowl car to unlock the gate, enter the service road on foot and stalk right in to inspect the sunken track & field, flashing that dinky–dick hand–held light all impotent cops are so invariably queer for! Or so I thought.

Rather than expose myself to the impotent cop I stealthily retreated to the lower southward end of the westward facing block of cement bleachers overlooking the stadium's frontward sunken tennis courts, making ready to slip out quietly by way of the rolled–back, chain–link construction fence if he descended down to the track & field as I figured he would. He never did.

Instead the impotent cop inexplicably trudged back and forth along the service road bordering the rear eastward side of the tennis court spectator stands, flashing his light all along the chain–link construction site fence and testing the security of the *inside* fence *gate*—ridiculously absurd since such a sizable section of the fence itself was readily rolled back!

Crouched at the cement steps at either end, I slinked from the lower southward to the upper northward end of those spectator stands and laid low, squatting to reconnoiter and spy his next move. Finally this clod of an impotent cop exited the service road gate, re–locking it.

I got to my feet and crossed the frontward construction site, slinking stealthily to the gate itself, pausing to peep gradually around a tall cement column—only to discover this impotent cop's prowl car *still* idling there! Literally just past the gate but a precious few feet away!

Quickly I crouched back down behind that cement

column just inside until I overheard the impotent cop report that gate "all secure," get into his prowl car and drive off.

I slipped right out through the rolled–back breach in the chain–link fence and left myself.

All secure indeed!

§

Friday night the 4th of August 1995 I was cavorting together with my comely young Korean–American mistress all over *Kroeber Hall* on the University of California campus at Berkeley; I was very familiar with that hall thanks to a pretty swing–shift Latina custodian working there whom I'd had an affair with in times past.

From the darkened lobby outside of the hall's *Phoebe A. Hearst Museum of Anthropology* we climbed the southward stairwell to the fourth–level landing, peeling off her panties and prying apart her sweet, thickset thighs so I could prick her soppy pussy right there atop the stone steps.

Afterwards we descended together to the northward, first–floor lecture hall auditorium, finding our way into the small midmost alcove separating the hall's sidelong doorways. Entry to the alcove was just inside the hall's rightward doorway. Luckily I locked the alcove door once we stepped inside.

Seating my comely Korean–American mistress atop the alcove's worktable with her legs spread wide open, I stood between her sweet, thickset thighs to resume pricking her soppy pussy.

Directly though we heard an impotent *Cal* campus cop—recognized by the sporadic squelch of his walkie–talkie—unexpectedly enter the hall, locking both of its doorways from inside. Next he roughly rattled the alcove's doorknob! Paralyzed by the dread of getting caught, we both froze, waiting with bated breath.

Through a puny peephole, I could barely make out the lumbering *Cal* cop, who descended to the foot of the inclined auditorium, grunting a lot aloud as he slouched and sprawled noisily on the bottom front–row spectator seats, fitfully flipping the pages of magazines or newspapers.

Relaxed, my mistress reclined supine across the tabletop. I stood nearby, softly shifting the position of my feet.

Breathless, we were stranded there on edge for roughly a full hour before the impotent *Cal* cop finally got to his listless feet and trudged out of the auditorium.

Presently we ourselves left undetected—going right out for super beef and chicken burritos to *La Burrita* at 2530 Durant Avenue in the Berkeley *Bog!*

§

Before it was ultimately acquired by *Starbucks* in late 1999 the shop located at 2128 Oxford Street in the Berkeley *Bog* was occupied by the San Francisco–based *Pasqua Coffee* retail chain that was called the *Pedestrian Café* once it opened its first single store in 1983.

By that time I'd traded in my comely young Korean–American mistress for a much bustier and far more beautiful if somewhat short Filipina–American mistress.

Saturday evening the 28th of August 1999 we met up with one another at *Pasqua Coffee*, situated at the corner intersection of Center Street, crossing together Oxford/Fulton Streets to the grassy and woodsy foot of

Cal campus in the midst of the Berkeley *Bog*'s so–called annual "summer blues festival," which was gratefully winding down.

That north fork of *Strawberry Creek*—the principal watercourse running through the Berkeley Bog—flows through the middle of *Cal* campus and partly through its foot at its *Eucalyptus Grove*, where I led her on by way of the curved, semicircular crescent drive of *Springer Gateway* to fool around in.

Following a narrow dirt footpath I led the way into a low–lying niche of a shrubbery–shrouded thicket of underbrush.

No sooner were we stripped and screwing in the bushes did a pair of *Cal*'s impotent campus keystone cops—one Asian, one black—come crouched, creeping and crunching sluggishly toward us through the brush-wood! Utterly un–*FUCK*–ing–believable!

"Hey! What are you doin' in there?" the black one accosts us.

"Just trying to make a little love," I answered him back. "Is there anything wrong with that?"

Frantically we'd already fumbled in the brush put-ting our clothes back on.

"It's against the law if I see it," he spouted, "but I'm not looking for you."

It turned out that dynamic duo of impotent campus keystone cops were after a skedaddling bunch of pot–smoking gutter punks.

"Good!" I exclaimed, relieved. "So do we have to go?"

"It would be a good idea since I've seen you," he dryly advised.

"Thank you," I said resignedly.

Utterly un–*FUCK*–ing–believable!

Well, that rude interruption didn't stop us from fuck-ing for long: past sunset I promptly led us to the north end of campus to the foot of the south side of *Cal's College of Engineering* administrative offices(*McLaughlin Hall*) where we romped to our genitalia's content amidst the soft, pine needle–covered, sweet–scented cedar foliage at the base of that building–a secret and special spot I was already well familiar with from past outdoor trysts!

§

If for that matter as a *Cal* student you've ever wondered where *UC Berkeley **Bog*** campus cops were *on*–campus if and when you've ever needed them, then it could very well be they were actually *off*–campus piddling around the lower northside of town, wrongly wasting time and effort rousting some non–student for some escaped or uncaught suspect's crime!

No joke I kid you not!

Early Monday morning well past midnight the 16th of June 1997 I was headed on foot for the northwest corner of Martin Luther King Jr Way(Old Grove Street) and Virginia Street where a pay phone was located.

Headlights suddenly flashed on from an idling *UC Berkeley* cop car, which abruptly barreled right over to the phone booth, lurching to a sudden stop—crossing the median of the street and facing head–on into the opposite lane, violating the right–of–way of any oncoming traffic and, of course, posing a dangerous traffic hazard to any car turning the corner there. Then the predictable spotlight beam glared blindingly in my face.

All impotent cops are quite queer for flashing their lights—whether dick–held or not—into people's faces—to say nothing of melodramatic but dangerous cop car maneuvers. They'll lamely claim it's for their own self–protection but in fact they really get off on its supposed shock effect—especially at night.

No doubt it was meant to frighten and intimidate me in this particular petty incident. Instead it just annoyed me as it invariably does.

My first fleeting thought: Oh God, here comes another jerk–off impotent cop out to prove his—or her—pseudo–machismo at somebody else's expense.

"Is that necessary?" I asked my impotent cop–flasher, getting no answer back. "Why are you shining that light in my face?"

And out of the cop car steps up this stumpy candidate for dyke prom queen, demanding my ID in this ridiculously pretentious he–woman tone of voice. Need I tell you how convulsively I was shivering in my shoes at that point?

Outright ignoring her(or he?)at first I went on dialing my pay phone number to listen to a theatrical hotline recording since I dabbled in acting at that time but had no home phone line for the moment.

"Get off the phone!" came her(or his?)next he–woman command.

"Then I want reimbursement for the change I'm losing for my incompleted toll call," I snapped, hanging up the phone. "What's your cause for detaining me?"

"Gimme your ID and I'll tell you," she(he?)retorted in her(his?)next pseudo–machismo display—doubtless to compensate for stunted growth!

Despite the daylight–intensity street lamps blazing overhead the he–woman cop still shined her dick–held flashlight on my ID to inspect it!

"You *look like* somebody who's broken into a car around here," she(or he?)finally stooped to tell me.

Having never met or seen me before in the light of day much less the dark of night(God and Heaven forbid!)—never mind the real culprit she(or he?)was supposedly after—please pause to grasp its full import:

that I *"look like"* some suspected car–breaker!

Now how the *FUCK* is she(or he?)supposed to know what either I or some unseen, uncaught suspect is supposed to look like? More, how the *FUCK* did this he–woman campus keystone cop ever even get commissioned much less—are you ready for this?—stitched with *sergeant's stripes?!*

No doubt for her intrepid crime–busting reputation for making her long line of felony arrests on the mean smutty streets of the Berkeley *Bog!*

By that time the he–woman cop radioed for brawnier back–up, presumably because she couldn't handle alone a peaceful, *off*–campus citizen trying to make an innocuous pay telephone call!

More melodramatic cop car maneuvers and up came an impotent Asian male cop after parking his cop car directly across the corner sidewalk facing his cop crony's car—then posing a two–fold traffic hazard!

Next came the tediously dull and dumb interrogations:

•"Where are you coming from?"(a cafe)
•"Where are you going?"(Again—to make a bloody phone call!)

As if anything I was or was about to do was any of their damned business! But I readily answered their stupid questions in the vain and futile hope I could get on about my *own* business sooner rather than later.

Wrong!

They'd wasted that much time letting their culprit get away so they might as well grant even more flight–time!

Next came the even stupider pants pat–down and coat–pocket search: done from behind me by the Asian cop as he lightly held with one hand each of my wrists, separately in turn while searching each opposite side of me with his free hand.

Next came the dullest and dumbest interrogation: "Do you have any *knives?*"

No, Dunce, I thought, but perhaps I could scare up an ax or hatchet or two!

Next came the request to search my backpack, which I consented to, hoping once more for an expedited end to the entire farcical charade. Wrong again!

"Certainly," I obliged, dropping my backpack to the ground.

Squatting at my feet like a voyeuristic little kid the Asian cop ransacked my entire backpack, including its front pocket, most obligingly peeling off its zipper catch.

"Meanwhile," I said pointedly, "while you're wasting your time doing that the real culprit you're after is getting long gone and away."

What really lit up the he–woman cop's smirking face—especially then that no evidence of any kind whatever was found that I'd committed any crime—was her(his?)computer records report of outstanding "warrants" out on me for two minor unpaid traffic tickets.

"We could take you to jail," she(he?)gloated, "but I'm going to give you a break on these warrants since you've been cooperative."

"And I'll continue giving you a break as long as you don't *make a fool of yourself,*" she(he?)added smugly—polite and professional to the end.

"What's that supposed to mean?" I asked the he–woman cop.

"What part don't you understand?" she(he?)answered my question with a question.

"Is that some sort of threat or bargain for certain behavior from me?"

"There's no threat," the Asian cop interjected since the he–woman cop couldn't answer for herself.

"Then why does she imply I would act like a fool?"

"She didn't," the Asian cop interjected again, lying outright in front of all three of us about what the he–woman cop had just said.

"Very well then," I said, taking out pen and paper from my backpack. "Let's write down what she said."

"You're giving me a break on these warrants *be-cause...*," I began, pausing to await a reply which never came.

"Do what you will," I told them both flatly after an awkward lull of quiet, making it quite clear that the he–woman's implied threat of arrest for traffic tickets would in no way affect or dictate my conduct or behavior.

We all knew exactly what she meant though: since I answered stupid questions I didn't have to answer—and consented to a silly search of my backpack I could've re-fused—she(he?)in all her magnanimous machismo was giving *me* a "break" I neither needed nor wanted, much less asked for.

Impotent cops are of course petty power–tripping control freaks and really get off on trying to frighten and intimidate the gullible and uninformed by mak-ing their picayunish points. And these two impotent crime–busting cop clods were no different.

"You *better* take care of those traffic tickets," they both chimed in, presuming to tell me how to handle my own personal business, dangling out before me the only thinking thing impotent cops know since reason and rationality are so foreign to them: the ever pervasive threat of force and punishment.

"Is there anything else you want from me?" the he–woman cop accosts me as if she(he?)had anything worthwhile to offer anyone.

"Just your name."

She finally recited to me her full name, prefacing it boldly and bravely with the word, "Sergeant!" She was self–importantly prouder of her title—which she likely earned through nepotism—than her own name. Really *bizarre!*

From the git–go our bungling he–woman heroine already made a fool of *herself*(himself?)and proved how incompetent *she*(he?)was by her demonstrably pre-sumptuous attitude that she'd cornered a guilty culprit without the slightest reasonable cause or evidence; by her(his?)childishly puerile, pseudo–macho—and out-right laughable—demeanor; and by her(his?)very bad judgment–call, instigating the whole senseless farce in the first place!

Worst of all, the poor victim of whatever actual crime these impotent cop clods exploited as their pre-text for rousting me surely saw no good or beneficial result come out of the farce.

SIX:

ALBANY'S FINEST, UPTIGHT NEANDERTHAL

Albany Hill is a bunchy hillock situated on the east shore of San Francisco Bay within the city confines of Albany, California, a tiny town in Alameda County sandwiched between Berkeley and El Cerrito. Overspread with native oak and non–native eucalyptus trees its hillsides are clustered with residential high–rises. A public park's perched upon its northern slope. Narrow winding roads turn and twist round its woodsy outer perimeter.

China Mandarin Airlines Flight 642 crashed due to pilot error at *Hong Kong International Airport* Sunday the 22nd of August 1999, killing three passengers—the very same day a mightily uptight impotent Neanderthal Albany cop actually took me into custody to cite me for(get *THIS!*)an *unpaid* San Francisco *traffic ticket five years old!* Actually it was primarily to appease his impotent exiguous ego!

§

If you haven't figured it out by now I'm a hardened, hard–core and incorrigibly corrupt criminal—rotten to my vile and evil core—and a dangerous menace to polite society at large! Good God, it's small wonder I haven't been branded *Public Enemy Number One* on every dangerous fugitive wanted list on the planet!

For that matter so should some of my girlfriends. Only I have no criminal record. Nor do I do any real harm or injury to anyone except perhaps offend the petty sensitivities of the prying, prudish and puritanni-cal. For that matter nor have my girlfriends.

Our wicked and sinful act? Our heinous and uncon-scionable crime? Our depraved and dastardly misdeed? Beware! It shall strike mortal terror into any faint heart: sometimes we've slept and—God and Heaven forbid—even screwed late at night on public streets in our legally parked car!

This allegedly lewd and lascivious conduct—this allegedly obscene and indecent behavior—is of picayunish importance to our intrepid impotent police, who run into hiding rather than fight truly violent crime committed against people and property by truly dangerous criminals in well–known, high–crime areas. That's why we steered clear of parking at equally well–known lovers' lanes, so–called, heading instead for residential neighborhoods, which our fearless impotent police purposely shy away from patrolling—for fear they might actually stop or deter burglars and robbers by their ever–so–formidable presence.

Bravest and boldest of all in taking a fanatical interest in intimately entwined couples steaming up parked cars proved to be the impotent Albany police: they're big, bad and smug—and they're out in force to protect and serve the community by making it safe for celibacy! In stark contrast with the impotent Berkeley *Bog* police making their community safe by harassing the homeless—their very own valiant specialty!

§

Our unsavory run–in with Albany's Finest and powerfully impotent police happened late Saturday night the 21st of August 1999 whilst we were resting beneath a blanket in the rear of my voluptuous Filipina–American mistress' hatchback car, parked on a winding road at the foot of the *Albany Hill Park* bluff behind a long row of legally parked cars close to some hillside apartments where we'd already parked numerous times before unmolested—until then! We'd rightly dismissed the circular hillcrest turnabout farther uphill as a conspicuous cop trap.

Our accosting impotent cop was bowling along dangerously up the narrow and steep grade in his prowl car, grinding to an abrupt halt once he caught a salivating glimpse of my girlfriend's ill–chosen phosphorescent blanket in passing. Impotent cops can drive recklessly and break speeding laws the rest of us get penalized for, you see—they're commissioned to set a good example and be role models for us all!

Impulsively he flashed us with the obligatory and ubiquitous spotlight that all impotent cops are so uncontrollably queer for, aspiring no doubt to get off on the cheap, voyeuristic thrill of watching two nubile teenagers making out in a rumble seat. Pity he missed it! We'd already done the nasty earlier!

Coming at us, swerving and screeching with all the melodramatic urgency of a *SWAT(Special Weapons and Tactics)*team onslaught, he was so soundly disappointed with the supreme let–down of finding instead two grown–up consenting adults, that all he had left to fall back on was his equally melodramatic demand for our IDs, exhorting us disparagingly that some nebulous and obscure city ordinance prohibited sleeping in cars. Who's *that* meant to protect besides greedy landlords cheated out of their exorbitant rents?

Now here was a courageous crime–buster really on the alert for dangerous criminals committing serious crimes! Of course his puny ego just couldn't stand being told by a citizen that he just might possibly have better and more important things to waste his time on in the performance of his impotent duties—whilst so dutifully protecting and serving the community. Of course his highly selective enforcement of the "law," which he lectured us about so condescendingly, conveniently ignored the fact that he's sworn first to uphold the US Constitution—including Free Speech and the Bill of Rights.

Hesanctimoniouslyblamedusfor"putting(ourselves) in the situation"—as if we'd invited him simply by being there to rudely intrude on our privacy and needlessly badger us. How ominously sinister a threat to society at large can one couple peacefully sleeping in a legally parked car pose, after all? So *WHAT* "situation?"

This particular court jester posing as an impotent cop was so thinly transparent in his petty intent he was outright laughable: he's plainly the breed of egomaniac who deludes himself to think, quite mistakenly, that wearing a badge, baton, gun and **Gestapo** uniform automatically entitles him to subservient deference and respect.

He most definitely displayed his festering jealousy of the mere fact that a beautiful voluptuous young woman would go along to do anything, anyplace with me by the sheer force of who I am, rather than by the barbaric brute force of overbearing boorishness like his, once he preached pompously that I would never bring her to such a place had I showed her any "respect."

Well, I never brought her, **DUNDERHEAD**—she brought *ME*, quite freely and willingly—in her own car to boot!

What the likes of this power–tripping control–freak sorely needs to learn is that commanding respect means first to *EARN* respect—not by coddling a minuscule ego falling far short of measuring up to the size of his witless nightstick, nor by abusing or misusing his self–serving authority, but by doing good and dealing fairly with people, and possibly even being of some small service and *USE* to the community he pretends to serve and protect. How utterly useless and ineffectual he must really feel to realize that he neither renders nor serves *ANY* purpose whatever by doing *NOTHING* on the job of any *REAL* importance or value!

Now over the past several years I'd been stopped whilst driving a girlfriend's car under various pretexts by accosting impotent cops from different departments: *Golden Gate Recreational Area(GGRA)*, Marin County and even UC Berkeley. *ALL* of them noted that an administrative "warrant" had been put out for me for a *five*–year–old *TRAFFIC TICKET* issued to me by a San Francisco motorcycle cop in **1994!** *NONE* of them *WASTED* roughly *THREE HOURS* or more of our time—shirking more pressing duties—to arrest, book and incarcerate me simply to issue me a fresh citation and notice to appear to pay my dated traffic ticket! This heroic comic posing as an impotent Albany peace officer *DID!* Why? As I commented even whilst being tightly handcuffed: ***PETTY SPITE!***

Packing me tight like the proverbial sardine into the hermetically sealed can in the back of his prowl car he barreled with me down the hill to the impotent cop station. Because I suffer from chronically inflamed and mucus–clogged nasal passages—and a deviated right septum—which make breathing difficult and laborious in such cramped and confined spaces, I nearly grew panic–stricken. His prisoner's cage was so narrow that I had to stretch out lengthwise because of my height just to fit into it. So airtight that I felt frightfully claustrophobic, which this *CLOD* of an impotent cop insisted stupidly was no "medical condition" whilst filling out wasted forms later on. My doctor would disagree.

Once he brought me into the station house cell block this impotent cop–*CLOD* locked me up first inside of a wooden cage, roughly the size of a telephone booth, having a hard bench to sit on. Through the heavy door of this oversized box he told me I could make three telephone calls to summon someone to pay my trivial traffic ticket bail of $179. I told him in turn that I would stay his guest for as long as he liked before I would bother anyone in the pre–dawn hours of the morning to trouble themselves over this farcical episode. So after he finally got it through his big fat blocked head that he'd *failed* to coerce me to pay any so–called "bail" by locking me up, he let me out, took off the handcuffs, confiscated my running shoes and sat me down after an overlong delay to drudge through superfluous paperwork—and "cite(me)out."

"This is all so petty," I'd told him, heaving a bored sigh.

"*DA, da, da, da*...judge didn't tink so," he stuttered, misguidedly thinking he'd made his clever comeback.

Funny, I hadn't seen any judge present at the scene of my latest crime's public–imperiling commission! In actual fact, my original judge—a gracious black gent—had actually *LOWERED* my original traffic ticket fine on appeal and had even gratefully *THANKED* me for coming into his court in the City! Late–fee penalties had raised the amount of my amended fine for my failure to pay at the time—solely out of my inability to pay, not deliberate or intentional evasion. But there was really no point in attempting to debate the irrelevant with the impotent ***IGNORAMUS!***

What struck me most whilst watching this bold *BUFFOON* plod through all his petty motions was my repeatedly thinking: now here's a great big but very bad walking–and–talking ***JOKE*** taking himself way too seriously! He was straining so strenuously to bluff and bluster all around the room he'd carted me to, trying in vain to puff up and strike a more menacing pose than he was ever capable of, he was actually *CREAKING* beneath the weighty burden of all the leathery, combat trappings weighing him down!

This frivolous traffic ticket arrest must have been the crowning *BIG BUST* of his whole worthless career!

He lumbered all around the room glaring at me—rigid, stiff and *EXTREMELY UPTIGHT*—trying ineptly to intimidate me to no avail. I simply stared him down with a quizzical look.

"Is something wrong?" he growled provocatively, scowling at me.

"No," I answered him back, shaking my head and simply smiling.

I *could* meet the challenge of his craven provocation *ANYTIME* he cared to quit *COWERING* behind the sissified skirts of a badge and the unequal protection of the "law"—something much too unrealistic to ever expect!

Finally he finished off his bogus sham of an arrest with the needless rigmarole of booking, finger–printing and—in a desperate, last–ditch, impotent attempt to aggravate and coerce me to cough up my "bail"—cooping me up for an overlong period in yet another but larger lockup. He was so absurdly and obsessively preoccupied with trying so ineptly to bully me that he forgot completely to photograph me. That final chore he left, embarrassingly, for some other impotent cop–crony who found me lying down and resting comfortably on the floor mat once he came at last to unbolt the clanging door and let me out.

§

Statisticians harp constantly that certain truly dangerous and violent crimes are committed everywhere by real felons every few minutes. What should thoroughly *infuriate* both citizens and politicians alike is that *any* impotent police department would fail so miserably to set and enforce strict *priorities* amongst its impotent cops for fighting and preventing really serious crimes! That any community would condone letting some impotent *BLOCKHEAD* cop get away with stroking his *PYGMY EGO* by arresting, handcuffing, booking and incarcerating *any* citizen on the silly pretext of a trifling traffic ticket is outright unconscionable!

Communities everywhere could effectively deter this sort of spineless shysterism amongst unscrupulous impotent cops by *PUBLISHING* and *PUBLICIZING* arrest records and clearance rates of crimes by type and severity.

Lengthy contact with *CHILDISH CHARACTERS* the likes of this impotent *ALBANY ASS* effectively dissuaded me from accepting a law enforcement commission myself in Florida years ago—even though I graduated from my police training "academy" with honors after earning as well both an AS degree in law enforcement and a BA degree in criminal justice. That ludicrous, laughable and all–too–frequent incident just reinforces my steadfast conviction that most impotent cops serve only to hinder(not help)people and protect mostly their own insecure egos over their unprotected communities.

If ever the dearly beloved one of some proverbial pillar of the community lay dying on some street someplace in a pool of their own blood—the victim of some dangerous felon's deadly and violent crime—then perhaps the crucial question would be eagerly posed: how many chivalrous impotent cops on the force were so earnestly and energetically engaged elsewhere at the time indulging their egos(or their voyeuristic perversions)by accosting couples sleeping peacefully in legally parked cars—or by arresting peaceful citizens for outstanding petty traffic tickets?

§

If you most mistakenly thought that one petty, harassment arrest by some blockheaded, pygmy–egoed
impotent cop would deter us from continuing to screw
in our legally parked car on public streets then *THINK
AGAIN!* It hadn't. It wouldn't.

If you don't care and couldn't give a flying hang
where we've been doing it then you gain great credit.
You shouldn't. Our only point is: nor should inept and
voyeuristic impotent cops!

§

Once more though that irresistible impulse to commit our ecstatic—but alas!—victimless crime struck
us one rare but bright, sunny and warm day early the
4th of December 1999 in the west Berkeley *Bog.* So we
headed further westward to the comforting–if–unmolested waterfront at the foot of Cedar Street, driving
to the end of a narrow "Not–A–Through–Street" road,
winding through some commercial district and ter-
minating at a construction site beneath some freeway
overpass. And naturally Big Brother–in–Blue would be
pervertedly watching!

Once more we'd rightly dismissed the secluded spot
underneath the overpass as the impotent cop trap it
turned out to be. So we parked instead beside a tall
hedge in a Saturday–vacant business building lot.

Unknowingly though we'd wandered into the grand
duchy of Albany, California where incompetent impotent cops try so ineptly to aggrandize themselves by
accosting amorous couples in cars! And before long

yet another gallant hero from amongst Albany's Finest had so cunningly hemmed us in our designated parking space from behind with his prowl car and promptly pestered us for no plausible purpose—except perhaps to investigate trespassing with intent to cast a car's hazardous shadow onto a defenseless and empty parking space!

These dauntless demigods simply have way too much downtime on their idle hands!

Forget his even asking whether we needed much less wanted his most untimely and unwanted assistance! He asked us instead how we were doing—as if we'd parked there well out of the way anxiously awaiting his undesired intrusion. We were doing fine, actually, enjoying a most pleasant and private conversation until he invited himself to so rudely interrupt and ruin it. So, was he out crime–busting or what?

Misguided by his own impotent police–instilled paranoia he automatically presumed us guilty until proven innocent, asking us whether we were committing any crime, having already intruded enough to inspect our car's interior—his true motive anyway—and see clearly that no contraband displayed itself in plain view. Did it look like we were committing any crime? Looks can be deceiving, he cracked.

Oh yeah, we were a couple of dangerous and violent felons in desperate and reckless flight to avoid prosecution for the steamy sex we'd just had in broad daylight some minutes before his late intrusion—parked there at a stationary standstill. We'd already done the nasty. What a pity he'd missed it! Nice to get the benefit of the doubt in any event.

Why ever he accosted us in the first place he never did say. Incompetent impotent cops in those parts are incapable of comprehending the concept of probable cause!

So we'd simply leave and be on our way—unless of course he meant to put us through the ridiculous rigmarole of checking our IDs, which we even volunteered to show him.

No, he gave us his overly generous permission to stay parked and sitting there—as if we'd ever needed it in the first freakin' place! How very *MAGNANIMOUS* of him—as if we were still in the mood to stay after he'd stuck his big, blocked, bulldog head through our window to bother us!

Leave peaceable people *alone, JERK–OFF!*

§

A footnote about the traffic ticket(**Co75349444– S**)dated Friday the 22nd of April 1994 issued to me by a stout, professional and business–like *San Francisco Police Department*(**SFPD**)motorcycle cop for expired vehicle registration and running red lights along the lengthy city's north–south drag, Van Ness Avenue, at the east–west side street, Sacramento. Those two traffic ticket fines amounted to a $239 combined legalized extortion; the red light infraction itself was fined $154.

"Your crime for the evening is not stopping for the red lights," he'd sedately advised me, sounding concerned. "Be careful."

Well, I appealed that citation at the Traffic Fines Bureau, Municipal Court, Room 101, Hall of Justice, San Francisco, Tuesday the 14th of June 1994 at 3PM— just two days after OJ Simpson slaughtered Nicole Brown Simpson and Ronald Goldman.

The kindly black judge presiding over my appeal dismissed outright the vehicle registration violation since the automobile wasn't owned by me but belonged to my Korean–American mistress and wasn't my personal responsibility.

As for the red light–running violation the judge stayed that fine to just $75(due Friday, 29 July 1994) after I argued successfully that I'd safely entered and crossed the intersection during the yellow caution light–change, not during the red light—otherwise I would've obstructed the teeming side–street traffic, which I hadn't.

Due to my poor financial condition and inability to pay I didn't send the $75 payment for the citation until Thursday the 22nd of December 1994. By Wednesday the 10th of August 1994 though the SFPD's Central Warrant Bureau issued an arrest warrant for me for the outstanding citation's "bail", which had been raised to the exorbitant extortion of $179—and which supplied the phony pretext for arrest by the impotent Neanderthal cop in Albany nearly to the month *FIVE YEARS* after the fact!

DA, da, da, da judge didn't tink so!

DA, da, da, da judge had actually *THANKED* me for attending his court!

So Wednesday the 1st of September 1999 I promptly sent the paid $179 extortion via postal money order to dispense with future pretexts for arrest by other impotent cops.

Even with the tacked on $104 late penalty fine I was still gratified that I'd saved $60 on appeal from my inability to pay that kindly judge's stay of the initial citation!

It's a nice neat little legalized extortion racket the police state of California runs all the same!

SEVEN:

RICHMOND'S FINEST, EXPERT PROFESSIONAL SHIRKER

Richard Colvin Reid, scuzzy incompetent Islamic fundamentalist "terrorist," was arrested Saturday the 22nd of December 2002 for attempting to blow up a commercial airliner in–flight by detonating with a match on *American Airlines Flight 63* his lame–ass "shoe bomb" supposedly composed of *PETN*(pentrite)plastic explosives. That very same night an intrepid impotent cop from the Richmond Police Department issued me a traffic ticket citation(**34–66210**)for driving an uninsured vehicle and for making an "improper right turn"—out of his jurisdiction in bordering El Cerrito, California!

§

The truth of the matter was I was driving along with my wife—with her permission—my *sister–in–law*'s car, accounting for the vehicle being "uninsured" in my name even though it was fully insured in hers; I *had* to drive because my wife wasn't even licensed to drive.

My wife's sister was in the process of moving all her belongings from an apartment in Marina Bay to a nearby storage space warehouse when she abruptly had to fly out of the country, traveling to Lima, Peru in South America. In the spirit of the Christmas season my wife and I were doing her sister the favor of removing the rest of her personal property from that apartment to storage. That Saturday night we were headed back to that Marina Bay apartment, making one last trip to pick up a dining table to keep at our place that couldn't fit with the rest of her sister's things in storage. Marina Bay's a residential waterfront community situated in the protected Inner Harbor of Richmond, California.

It's called doing a **GOOD TURN** for somebody, officer, you really ought to try it sometime whilst on "duty!"

§

We were driving leisurely along the north–south drag called San Pablo Avenue, approaching the El Cerrito del Norte(*del Norte* or "north hillock" for short) BART station—the second of two such BART(Bay Area Rapid Transit)stations in El Cerrito, California just east of the murderous 6400 Cutting Boulevard interchange of Interstate 80(I–80).

Stopped at a red light at San Pablo Avenue and the side street, Hill, we found ourselves facing the tail end of a sluggish and overlong Gestapo "sobriety checkpoint," so–called—those arbitrary, capricious and un-constitutional(outlawed in 11 states)conveyor belt–like roadblocks whereby impotent cops stop and "process" at a snail's pace every last car passing through it, aspir-ing to rack up traffic ticket extortion points under the pretext of preventing drunk drivers(more easy marks).

If these oh–so–caring–and–concerned impotent cowardly crime–busting cops really aspired to save lives then why haven't they ever set up **MURDER** checkpoints in known high violent crime areas like that nearby Cutting Boulevard, where countless homicides have occurred in Richmond, California over the years?! Because the marks aren't so easy there and these chick-en–shit impotent cops are too cowardly and afraid even to patrol such areas, that's why!

Admittedly a very bad move on my part—but spurred by the fact that there wasn't even a single, solitary ve-hicle idling or approaching from behind us—I turned off right from the *left* lane of San Pablo Avenue onto sidewise Hill Street, hoping to bypass that impotent cop "sobriety checkpoint." And *not* because I was ei-ther drunk or had anything to hide, which I hadn't! So it was indeed an "improper"(albeit safe)right turn and

I'd pay the price for it.

NAILED! No sooner did I complete my "improper right turn" did I see him—the impotent Richmond cop sitting on his spineless ass in his prowl car parked in the lot of the del Norte BART station—out of his jurisdiction—in El Cerrito, California! Naturally the swirling lights flashed on and he swerved and screeched to melodramatically pull over and stop our creeping car in "hot pursuit."

Unbeknownst to me my driver's license had been administratively *"suspended"* by the California DMV effective as far back as 9 August 2000—over a full calendar year previous—for non–payment of that "lighting during dark" citation(**Docket #: 918–841–7**)issued to me the 13th of February 2000 by that impotent Berkeley *Bog* cop named **Salas** for verbally offending his exiguous ego. Despite the attempted legalized coercion that particular traffic ticket extortion **remained** **un**paid until it went off my driving record altogether by 2005. Like I said, I don't pander to the exiguous egos of impotent cops.

So this impotent Richmond cop sitting on his spineless ass in **EL CERRITO** nearly soaked his orgasmed pants, getting off on confiscating my driver's license and issuing me a pink slip "verbal notice" of my driver's license suspension, which until that moment I honestly hadn't a clue about since I normally never drove anyway. At the same time he smugly issued me the traffic ticket citation(**34–66210**)for supposedly driving uninsured whilst making my "improper right turn."

Why did I turn right off the road to begin with was the impotent cop's first retardate question.

"Because you're *blocking the road!*" I barked back.

I duly owned up to the turn infraction and paid its exorbitant traffic ticket fine of $124 after receiving in the mail this "reminder notice" of legalized coercion: *"FAILURE TO PAY, APPEAR OR COMPLY by 04/05/02, will result in one or more of the following: imposition of a civil assessment increasing the amount due to $921.00 and your case being referred to a collection agency; Notification to Department of Motor Vehicles to suspend or refuse to renew your driver's license; And/or, issuance of a warrant for your arrest."*

This intrepid impotent Richmond cop reprimanded me for my "attitude" for doing nothing more than shaking my head and groaning in disgust whilst ordering me to park the car at the nearest curb and not drive it anyplace further—even though he could've permitted us to drive it home to our apartment complex a mere few blocks away within a comfortable walking distance. No, he reveled in maximizing our inconvenience—our just reward for doing somebody a good turn at Christmastime.

"No attitude," I told him point–blank in parting, "I just sincerely hope you find something more important to do out there."

"This is as important as it gets," he cracked with what he most mistakenly thought was a clever wiseacre comeback.

"I figured as much," I answered him right back, nodding knowingly.

He had no further impotent retort to that.

In 2004 Richmond was statistically the second most dangerous city in California, surpassing Oakland and was named the 8th most dangerous city in the country. Now Richmond ranks as the third most dangerous in California behind Compton and Oakland and 11th most dangerous nationally according to the Morgan Quitno rankings. For every 100,000 people there were 38.3 murders, 50.4 rapes, 485.8 robberies, 512 assaults,

1110.7 burglaries, 3497.4 counts of larceny and 2471.4 thefts of vehicles. Richmond had 42 murders in 2006; and the city suffered a record number of 62 homicides in 1991.

Here in December 2001 two days before Christmas day is this intrepid impotent Richmond cop sitting on his spineless ass in *EL CERRITO* at a citizen–harassing "sobriety checkpoint," boasting that patrolling his own crime–ridden jurisdiction is of no importance!

EIGHT:
EL CERRITO'S FINEST DUCHY POLICE

The imperious duchy of *El Cerrito*(Spanish for "little hill"), California is a suburban city located in Contra Costa County in the San Francisco *East* Bay Area. Its bordered to the north by black crime–ridden Richmond, California and to the west by the so–called *Albany Hill* where Albany's finest uptight neanderthal would daringly arrest me for an outstanding San Francisco traffic ticket! Running through the duchy is the destructive earthquake–prone Hayward Fault geologic Zone. It it has two BART(Bay Area rapid transit) stations: El Cerrito del Norte to the north and El Cerrito Plaza to the south. At the south-ward station is situated the El Cerrito Plaza shopping center—connected by an access ramp to the so–called *Ohlone Greenway*'s adjoining bicycle and pedestrian pathways stretching beneath the elevated BART tracks from the Berkeley *Bog* to Richmond.

By December 1999 I was living along with my wife in an apartment complex adjoining an office of California's Department of Motor Vehicles(DMV)locat-ed at 6400 Manila Avenue roughly one mile away from the El Cerrito Plaza. El Cerrito itself's roughly five miles from the University of California's *Cal* campus in the nearby Berkeley *Bog*—to and from which I'd routinely commute by train to work out at the so–called "down-town" Berkeley *Bog* YMCA. And as was my wont I'd typically hike, power–walk or otherwise stride on foot at all hours of the day or night that pedestrian pathway whenever returning from the *Bog* to El Cerrito, disem-barking at El Cerrito Plaza to traverse that mile–long stretch of pathway to the nearby DMV. I christened that trail simply the train trestle footpath!

As was their wont late at night the local yokel impo-tent cops for the imperious duchy of El Cerrito would routinely cruise in their prowl cars the broader asphalt bicycle path of the *Ohlone Greenway.*

§

Late Sunday night the 11th of March 2001 I was returning to our apartment, striding on foot the train trestle footpath, when I was randomly accosted and detained by a skulking impotent cop from the El Cerrito duchy police, cruising the bike path in his prowl car!

Without the first pretext of probable cause—unless striding the footpath late at night in the absence of any curfew constitutes probable cause—this impotent cop demanded my ID and rattled off at me his asinine and inane interrogations:

•"Where do you live?"

•"Where are you coming from?"

•"Where are you going?"

What the *FUCK* business is it of yours, I was thinking!

"Where do *you* live?" I finally asked *him* in turn.

His telling retort:

"That's *confidential.*"

Precisely, retardate!

§

Where the impotent cops of the imperious duchy of El Cerrito really excel and really shine is in their dauntless and fearless crime–busting rousting of penniless homeless people or paying shoppers pushing shopping cart baskets along the *Ohlone Greenway*'s bicycle and pedestrian pathways!

Wednesday night the 2nd of November 2005 I was crossing Manila Avenue from the DMV, pushing a loaded shopping cart recruited unavoidably from the nearby

Safeway chain supermarket store located roughly two blocks away from our apartment complex. Situated next to our apartment complex was the El Cerrito city impotent cop station itself located at 10940 San Pablo Avenue. Separating a part of the apartment complex and the impotent cop station was a narrow two–lane, dead–end side street—onto which an impotent cop was turning in his prowl car, headed for the impotent cop station. At that very moment I was crossing the avenue that night with the shopping cart he spotted me.

Melodramatically the impotent cop flashed me with his spotlight, turned about and doubled back in hot pursuit of me on foot! Already I was coasting with the shopping cart toward our apartment building block. Promptly the impotent cop caught up and overtook me on foot at breakneck speed in his speedy prowl car.

"How are 'ya doin'?" the impotent cop accosted me.
"Yes?"
"Do you live here?"
"Yes, I do."
"Are you going to take that cart back?"
"I didn't take it—I found it on the footpath."

It was shopping basket from the specialty chain grocery store, *Trader Joe's*, located roughly a mile away at the southward El Cerrito Plaza; I found the cart already abandoned nearby on the train trestle footpath and re-cruited it to transport several heavily–loaded grocery bags I was weighed down lugging and trudging home with.

"No, I'm not taking it back," I replied finally.

"All right," the impotent cop conceded, braking a bit before giving it up and driving off.

Now was that an exercise in crime–busting futility or what?

NINE:
PEEPING
PARK
POLICE

Perched on the headlands atop the bluffs at the westward edge of San Francisco, overlooking *Seal Rock* and the ruins of *Sutro Baths*, is the historic *Cliff House* restaurant—acquired and operated by the *National Park Service* since 1977 when it became part of the *Golden Gate National Recreation Area(GGNRA)*. *Seal Rock* is a huge, prominent rock bulging offshore at that northward end of *Ocean Beach*. Today the site of the historic *Sutro Baths*, once an enormous indoor swimming pool complex, lays in razed ruins consisting mostly of weatherbeaten cement walls, passageways, stairways and tunnels. It's one of my favorite corners of the world—and impotent cops out to fuck up your enjoyment of it abound!

§

My comely young Korean–American mistress and I'd just returned to her car after drinks late that Sunday night the 13th of March 1994 at the *Cliff House*'s cozy and comfy hunting lodge–style lounge—long before it was "modernized" and made over into the marbelized mausoleum it is today. Her car was quite legally parked in a darkened, non–metered, pavement–marked space in the designated asphalt lot situated a short distance up the sloping grade off *Point Lobos Avenue*. Chilling out there in her parked car I was getting my dick most satisfactorily sucked through my open zipper when this impotent park cop barreled up, blocking us in the space from behind and flashing us with his prowl car's blindingly bright spotlight. Naturally he shined us with his dinky–dick, hand–held flashlight they're all so queer for as well.

I sat in the driver's seat so my ID was demanded together with her car's registration, which had just expired at the end of the previous January—providing the impotent cop with his pretext for harassing us further.

"Are we breaking the law or are you just out voyeuring?" I'd asked, conspicuously perturbed.

"You looked *suspicious* parked in a *secluded spot* at this hour," he equivocated. "And I'd appreciate it if you didn't call me a voyeur."

If the flat–foot shoe fits! "Suspicious" how? A parking lot space's "secluded?"

"Is there a curfew here?"

No warning signs restrict parking lot time.

"We've had a lot of *criminal activity* out here," he equivocated further.

"Like what?"

"A lot of stolen cars."

Our car wasn't stolen.

"What's a guy from Berkeley(my ID's address)doing *making out* in San Francisco?"

Trying to fucking *enjoy* myself, preferably without interruption by some impotent peeping Tom? What the *FUCK* business is it of his where I make the *FUCK* out? Were there designated make–out zones located around the San Francisco Bay Area or what?

"We just came from the Cliff House," I replied simply. "I would've thought people parking in the restaurant lot would be pretty common."

"How old are you?" he asked, sounding surprised at my answer of 40 as I looked, yes, considerably younger.

"Maybe I should give you a ticket for not having a current registration..." he came on with the extremely predictable insinuated threat. And for what? Sheer envy my dick was getting the blow–job from a fresh and ripe young Asian chick his wasn't!

If giving us a ticket will give you a reason for being, I was thinking, but kept quiet to spare the chick the ticket; she couldn't find her paperwork in her cluttered glove compartment anyhow.

"Not me," I promptly corrected him. "It's *her* car."

"I'm going to have to ask you to leave the park," he said resignedly. "I won't write you a ticket if you leave the park."

That impotent cop wouldn't write *me* a ticket because it wasn't *my* car.

Ordered to leave by an impotent cop not the "park" but rather a lawfully employed ***PARKING LOT!***

Utterly un–*FUCKING*–believable!

§

Sunday night the 15th of October 1995 I ran whilst my comely young Korean–American mistress drove through San Francisco's *Golden Gate Park* to meet up again at *Ocean Beach* at the park's westward end. As was my wont I ran by way of the park's North Drive, renamed *John F. Kennedy Memorial Drive* after the Kennedy Assassination, winding from the park's eastward end to the *Great Highway.* From the historic Victorian wood–and–glass paned *Conservatory of Flowers* botanical greenhouse, I traditionally ran roughly three miles past the Dutch–style north windmill located at the park's extreme westward end, where she'd park at the curb nearby awaiting my arrival on foot.

After getting back behind the wheel in her car that night, I paused to look through my packet of consumer coupons in anticipation of visiting the nearby Ocean Beach *Safeway* chain supermarket store at 850 La Playa Street.

Whilst we idled there two impotent *Golden Gate National Recreation Area(GGNRA)*cops passed us by from the front on our left, promptly turning around to pull up and park their prowl car behind to accost us—for absolutely no probable cause as per usual!

Abruptly I opened out the driver's door in anticipation of the harassing encounter.

"Shut the door!" this familiar pseudo–macho New–*York*er impotent cop barked as he approached, flashing his hand–held dinky–dick light.

"The window doesn't roll down!" I snapped back. "What's wrong with you?"

"What's wrong with *me?*" he asked, aghast.

"Yes! What do you want? Why are you detaining me here? And why are you flashing that light in my face?"

"Because you're blocking the roadway and it's dark out," his supervising partner hastily interjected.

Traffic was utterly nil and we were pulled over snugly to the rightward curb.

"Why are you stopped here?"

"We're looking at supermarket coupons. Anything wrong with that?"

"That's fine. Is everything all right? Why are you sweating?"

"I just finished running."

"Then move this car from here before I give you a citation!" he threatened—likewise as per usual.

"I'll be happy to!" I retorted, slamming the car door shut and driving off.

§

Overlooking the razed ruins of the *Sutro Baths*(once a fabulous indoor swimming pool complex)—today weatherbeaten concrete walls, barricaded passageways and stairs and a tunnel ruptured by a deep crevice—is an elevated parking lot vista point situated atop a steep, sloping and blustery bluff, commanding a panoramic view of the *Cliff House, Seal Rock* and the expansive Pacific Ocean. The site of those battered baths are nowadays part of the *Golden Gate National Recreation Area(GGNRA)*and operated by the *United States National Park Service.*

Sunday evening the 25th of May 1997 on Memorial Day weekend I sat relaxed in the driver's seat of the car belonging to my comely young Korean–American mistress, whom I was watching feed snacks to a friendly and ravenous raccoon at the bluff's brink nearby. Her car was quite legally parked in a long row of multiple other cars parked for the holiday, looking out on the spectacular vista.

Before long this supreme punk of an impotent park cop crept up from behind in his prowl car, stopping and blocking in her car against the bluff's abrupt brink. Then he got out to approach and accost me.

"Oh no," I groaned audibly.

"Is there somethin' wrong?" cracked the cocky impotent punk cop. "Are you not feeling too well?"

I was feeling just fine before he imposed his ugly and unwanted face upon my peace and quiet.

"You make me *tired*," I groaned again with an extremely exasperated tone.

"Maybe you outta go out there and get some fresh air," cracked the cocky impotent punk cop, gesturing to the nearby bluff. "Are you gonna be alright?"

Maybe he outta go out there and take a flying leap off the bluff, I thought automatically.

"Yeah, I'll be fine once I get home, thanks," I answered him back tersely. "What do you want?"

Two verbal exchanges had transpired and the cocky impotent punk cop *still* hadn't stated any probable cause or reason why for his intrusive imposition!

"Do you have a current registration for this car?" he finally asked at last!

"I don't know," I groaned again, gesturing to my comely Korean–American mistress to come back to her car. "I'm not driving."

I promptly moved over to the car's passenger seat as my comely Korean–American mistress retrieved from her glove compartment her car's registration certificate, which was expired.

Going round the front of her car to meet the cocky impotent punk cop and hand over her car's registration, she then sat down in the driver's seat at his commanding direction. Next she fumbled in her purse for her driver's license, dropped it but picked it up before the cocky impotent punk cop could bend down to retrieve it himself.

"I was going to pick that up for you," cracked the cocky impotent punk cop, "*nice* guy that I am!"

Next he demanded my driver's license as well.

"I don't have mine," I lied to his manifest disbelief even though it was stashed in my wallet in my backpack..

The cocky impotent punk cop went briefly to his parked prowl car and directly returned, accosting *me* instead of her for her expired auto registration!

"Are you *Joseph Covino Jr*?" he badgered me. "Is that *you*?"

"Yes."

"Your name's connected with an outstanding warrant for another traffic citation for a 1995 expired registration," he charged accusingly.

"It's not my car," I said drearily.

"It don't matter," he persisted. "You're responsible for the state of the car so long as you drive it."

"No," I contradicted him, "I'm not responsible for a

car I don't own and doesn't belong to me."

"You're not getting it," cracked the cocky impotent punk cop.

"Oh, I get it," I retorted bluntly. "I just disagree with it and won't pay it."

"You could get arrested for a criminal offense," he bluffed and blustered badly.

"*Criminal?*" I asked, aghast.

"Well, no, not criminal," he equivocated, correcting himself.

"Oh!" I exclaimed mockingly. "I've been reprieved! So what do you mean by arrest?"

"Taken in and cited to appear. "Do you want to be taken in?"

"Go ahead," I challenged him wearily. "Do what you will if it'll make you feel good."

"Nice boyfriend you've got there," the cocky impotent punk cop cracked to my comely Korean–American mistress.

"I just don't understand your attitude," the cocky *retardate* as well as impotent punk cop cracked directly to me, going off and presently coming back.

"My attitude," I bluntly clarified, "comes from wondering when your last felony arrest was."

"Oh yeah," the cocky impotent punk cop bragged, swaggering. "I do all kinds of good stuff like that—like recently arresting a man with a gun."

"Great," I scoffed facetiously. "So have you ever helped anybody, saved somebody's life or done *anything* important?"

"And what do *you* do?" he asked me pointedly, nodding all the while. "*Nuthin'!*"

"Oh yeah!" I retorted just as pointedly—and sarcastically. "You're a real *hero!* Well, can we go now, Mister *Hero?*"

"Yeah, I think so," he retorted derisively—incapable of any other scurrilous comeback.

Well, we certainly didn't care to keep this intrepid cocky impotent punk cop from protecting the rest of that perfectly peaceful holiday parking lot ever so bravely!

Going off and coming back once more for the last time he finally—at long last—issued my comely Korean–American mistress a traffic citation for *her* expired auto registration instead of harassing me!

Well, what I didn't *do* was waste my time and effort pestering peaceful people in a fucking parking lot over the Memorial Day holiday weekend!

At that overtly expressed sentiment my young Korean–American mistress and myself slapped both upraised palms, high–fiving each other!

That cocky retardate impotent punk cop was finally and at long last *GONE*—the very same New–*Yorker* jerk–off who'd harassed us in *Golden Gate Park* nearly two years before in October 1995!

TEN:

MARIN

COUNTY

COP

PROFESSIONALS

Cops policing affluent, New Age Marin County, situated in the north San Francisco Bay Area across the Golden Gate Bridge from the city, have proved in my experience to be amongst the most gratifyingly polite and professional cops I've ever encountered anyplace.

§

Late Saturday night the 22nd of April 1995 I drove off along with my comely Korean–American mistress from a *Denny's* chain restaurant diner in Corte Madera("chopped wood" in Spanish), California, an incorporated town in Marin County, following a cop prowl car on our way. Following us was another prowl car cop trawling for drunk drivers recovering at the diner from making the rounds of the bars; he promptly pulled us over at random, explaining no probable cause for the inexplicable traffic stop.

I cracked open the driver's door since the driver's power window was inoperative, stuck in its up position and couldn't be lowered.

"Stay in the car and roll down the window!" the cautious cop commanded.

"I can't roll down the window," I announced.

"Then stay in the car and leave the door open!"

"That's what I'm doing."

He demanded the obligatory driver's license and vehicle registration.

"Is this your car?"

"No—hers. Would you like to see her driver's license to match it with her registration?"

"No. I need to see your driver's license since you're driving."

"Where are you going?"

"Berkeley."

The prowl car cop we followed out of the diner parking lot idled nearby to observe and oversee the stop.

"Have you been drinking?"

"Coke."

"Any alcohol?"

"No. Do I act like I've been drinking?"

Then he conducted the stupidest sobriety test: holding up a pencil in front of my face and ordering me to watch the tip of it, following along with my eyes—which I exaggeratedly bulged with a marked smirk—without turning my head as he moved its eraser from left to right.

So keenly clever these super sharp cops!

He cautioned us that the vehicle's license tag was missing its smog check sticker, invalidating the vehicle registration.

"I won't issue you a citation since it's not your registration," he announced.

"Thanks very much," I responded dryly.

"Have a nice day!" he declared mechanically, taking off as quickly as he'd come.

§

Late Friday night the 8th of September 1995 I was driving once more with my comely Korean–American mistress, exiting eastbound U.S Route Highway 101 headed for the 5.5–mile, double–deck *Richmond–San Rafael Bridge*(the *John F. McCarthy Memorial Bridge*), the so–called "roller–coaster span" which has been compared to a "bent coat–hanger," stretching over the northernmost east–west crossing of San Francisco Bay.

At Larkspur, north of San Francisco in Marin County, we decided to return southbound to neighboring Corte

Madera to stop at its *Denny's* chain restaurant diner.

No sooner did I make my perfectly safe U–turn beneath the Highway 101 to re–enter the freeway did yet another Marin County cop, trawling likewise for weekend drunk drivers, pull us over for a superfluous traffic stop.

"Roll down the window!" he brusquely ordered from outside.

"It doesn't roll down!" I announced, throwing open the door, stepping out but staying seated as I handed over my driver's license.

He stepped back to my left rear—that standard impotent cop vehicle–stop position.

"You can cut the police precautions," I reassured him facetiously. "I promise I won't shoot you."

"You need to calm your attitude."

"I don't have an attitude."

"I don't know you."

"I'm Joseph Covino Jr," I introduced myself, gesturing to the driver's license he was intently inspecting. "How do you do?"

"Did you know you made an illegal U–turn?"

"No."

"Did you see the sign prohibiting U–turns?"

"No."

"Where are you from?"

"Berkeley."

"Where are you coming from"

"Larkspur."

"Where are you going?"

"Denny's."

"Have you been drinking tonight?"

"No, I don't drink—and drive."

"I won't cite you," he announced magnanimously, "but observe the sign the next time."

"Thank you, I appreciate that," I said gratefully. "I honestly didn't see the sign."

"It's about three–by–five feet," he advised, motioning its dimensions. "Be careful getting back on the freeway."

Speedily he took off in hot pursuit of a passing motorcyclist.

§

Larkspur is a city in Marin County located north of San Francisco near Mount Tamalpais. Late Friday night the 31st of October 1997 my comely young Korean–American mistress and I were bound for the northernmost, 5.5–mile east–west, double–deck *Richmond–San Rafael Bridge*, and the East San Francisco Bay beyond, after having gone to the *Lark Theater* at 549 Magnolia Avenue to watch a Halloween revival screening of the bomb "horror–romance" movie dud, director Francis Ford Coppola's *Bram Stoker's Dracula(1992)*. Presently we were stopped by a Larkspur cop named Horowitz; I was driving us.

"I have to open the(driver's)door because the window won't roll down," I duly cautioned the already cautious cop. "What did I do?"

"Your rear lights are hazardously malfunctioning when the car's braked and your registration is recorded as expired," he explained simply.

Predictably the cop put us through that whole tedious and tiresome driver's license–registration–and–insurance paperwork rigmarole.

"I'll figure it out," he assured me, taking the haphazard pile of paper I handed him.

"I have to tell you," I alerted him, "my driver's license is expired too. I'm only driving because she's tired and feeling unwell."

"Why did you let your driver's license lapse?" he asked me.

"Because I don't drive," I clarified. "I don't even own a car."

"Here's the deal," the cop magnanimously admonished us after going off and coming back, "I'm not giving you a ticket even though you're operating this car totally illegal. Repair the rear lights. Let her sober up from being drunk and let her drive before being a Good Samaritan."

"She's not drunk," I corrected him. "We haven't been drinking. So it's wrong to assume that."

"Actually," she moaned, leaning over from the passenger seat to listlessly lift up her eyes to the cop, "I have *mono.*"

Mono—as in the infectious mononucleosis otherwise known colloquially as the "kissing disease."

In our special case it could very well've been called the fucking disease!

"Stop and throw water on her face to freshen her up to drive then," the cop brilliantly recommended.

"What's the penalty for driving without a license?" I asked him ironically. "There's a penalty for everything, I'm sure."

"There's a citation and a fine," he confirmed.

"Thanks for your help," I said appreciatively as he turned on his heel to return to his prowl car.

And we were off.

§

In the winter of 1963, **MR CLEAN**—with his imposing bald head, earring, folded muscular arms and strong, silent type but smiling demeanor—most fittingly portrayed a police officer "Grime–fighter" who really arrested dirt problems, and then in the spring of 1966 portrayed a "two-fisted grime–fighter," who knocked out dirt with one hand and left the shine with the other.

Late Saturday night the 7th of August 1999 I would experience an up close–and–personal encounter with the *black **Mr Clean*** cop of Tiburon, California!

Tiburon's an incorporated town in Marin County, occupying most of the Tiburon Peninsula, which stretches south into the San Francisco Bay. Contiguous with Tiburon is the smaller city of Belvedere, occupying the south–east part of the peninsula about four miles north of San Francisco. Tiburon's bordered by Corte Madera to the north and Mill Valley to the west but is otherwise surrounded by the Bay.

State Route 131(SR 131)is a state highway in Marin County, a short route connecting U.S. Route 101 with Tiburon. Its eastern terminus ends at the intersection with Tiburon's Main Street, turning into ***Paradise Drive***, a winding route which turns and twists around the eastern side of Tiburon Peninsula, leading ultimately to Corte Madera.

By that time I'd traded in my comely young Korean–American mistress for a much bustier and far more beautiful if somewhat short Filipina–American mistress, whom I'd already been bonking late that night in her car parked in a northward–facing turnout on *Paradise Drive*, where I'd frequently fucked the Korean–American chick during our numerous car excursions of times past.

After humping we'd laid down her hatchback's two rear seats, overspreading them with blankets and pillows though I was too tall and my limbs too long to recline comfortably(even crosswise)myself. She on the other hand snoozed and snored blissfully!

Out of comfort–seeking desperation I placed a pillow atop the leveled emergency brake and stretched out my torso between the car's two front seats, stretching out my legs lengthwise in the hatchback's rear. So I was finally sprawled shirtless between the two halves of her hatchback when we were abruptly flashed by a cop prowl car's bright and blinding spotlight.

First the intruding prowl car drove by, shining that spotlight on us in passing, but promptly turning around on the narrow two–lane road and doubling back to park behind and throw that blazing spotlight directly upon us.

Before long the bald and black **Mr Clean** cop stepped up and stuck both his scary face and dinky–dick flashlight through the open driver's window.

"Yes?" I asked nonchalantly.

"How are ya doin', pardner?" he greeted me. "What's goin' on?"

"Just trying to sleep."

"We're too tired to drive!" my panty–less girlfriend abruptly blurted out aloud from beneath her muffling blanket.

"Are you traveling?" the bald, black cop asked.

"We were."

"What's your destination?"

"The East Bay."

"We have an ordinance against people sleeping in their cars," he informed us.

"You've got to be kidding," I cracked, chuckling aloud. "This is Tiburon. Whaddya expect?"

"Do you want us to leave?"

"No, go back to sleep."

"Thank you."

Gee, it was just like receiving a summary Papal dispensation!

He flashed his light across us a little further before finally leaving to drive off.

Short, sweet and surprisingly professional! Bravo, **Mr Clean!**

ELEVEN:

WALNUT

CREEK'S

FINEST,

WAY

TOO

MUCH

DOWNTIME!

Well, the impotent paragon of police states is most certainly alive and well in Walnut Creek, California!

In late 2007 I received a voicemail message requesting contact from one impotent Creek cop, **Greg Thompson**, whose call I promptly returned out of compelling curiosity more than anything, as I'm no law-breaker and couldn't conceivably imagine what any impotent cop would be doing calling me.

Most mistakenly, I thought that no local police state canton could surpass duchy El Cerrito's theatre-of-the-absurd police antics of rousting pedestrians pushing shopping carts on the Ohlone Greenway—just as I never thought it even thinkable that you could get rousted by penny ante cops right at home without ever stepping outside of your apartment—but in this petty case the Creek not only excelled but exceeded all conceivable bounds of absurdity before my relocation there's aged even two years!

Thompson was calling on behalf of one **S. Chan**, a female Creek endodontist, whose office police "dispatch" had summoned him to handle a "threatening letter" complaint. Chan, Thompson claimed, asked him to "relay the message" to me that she wanted nothing to do with me, and wanted to receive neither letters nor telephone calls from me, and further, should I ever appear on her office property at La Casa Via in the Muir medical complex, that she herself would execute my citizen's arrest for "trespassing."

Now there's a pretty preposterous picture, seeing how this presumably powerfully paranoid woman and I have never, ever even *met* much less exchanged either in person, over the telephone or otherwise the first utterances of human communication with one another! Nor had she ever received the first "letter" from me, "threatening" or otherwise.

Chan had however just received from me via first class mail a simple flat parcel containing nothing but a *copy of a memo* attached to a combined two-part, six-page report composed by me referencing what I've termed "Shyster Dentistry Practices in the San Francisco East Bay Area." The memo and its accompanying report were addressed not to Chan but to both the Delta Dental of California insurance company and the state Dental Board of California, for their information, for strictly regulatory purposes.

As the memo itself clearly indicates, the report mentions multiple dental offices—and strictly as a "COURTESY"—copies of the report were posted to all those dental offices named. In effect, then, this document is a quite legitimate piece of purely business correspondence posted to multiple business offices. Chan freaked out, apparently, as her office was one of those ever so briefly and exactly mentioned thus—in its entirety:

§

"Then I referred myself due to close proximity to one **S. Chan**, whose *snooty-fruity* Latina receptionist only grudgingly made me an endodontist appointment after confirming that my dental plan insurance coverage allowed for not just one but two specialist consultations per year—the first having just been royally wasted with Dr. Bruns. When I promptly arrived right on that time for that particular appointment I found the solid, unwelcoming wooden door to Chan's office soundly locked! I knocked lightly and, receiving no response, commenced walking away when the *snooty-fruity* Latina receptionist, having leisurely sauntered out from behind her desk, belatedly opened up the office door.

"Conspicuously expecting to see a more elderly and perhaps even decrepit patient, Chan's *snooty-fruity* Latina receptionist stood aghast, looking down her nose at me from head to toe since I look roughly ten years younger than my actual chronological age from being an exceptionally fit and healthy practitioner of classic physical culture. 'Do you have an appointment?' she haughtily asked. Once I confirmed my name she led the way into the waiting room, sauntered leisurely back behind her desk and handed me a clipboard with forms to fill out. 'There's three pages,' she took profound pains to point out.

"Another patient directly departed from the office and the *snooty-fruity* Latina receptionist herself presently disappeared to someplace in the rear to audibly chit-chat with Chan, who'd poked her head out to take a quick peek at me filling out the forms—the third page of which contained obnoxious clauses as avaricious as anything her fellow endodontist, F. Bashiri, could've ever conceived: outrageous charges for cancelled or missed appointments and upwards of $1500 in "estimated" fees for a single root canal for which Dr. M. Min had charged a mere $870 less than a decade earlier. Miffed that I'd already wasted an inordinate amount of time filling out the first two pages of forms before getting to the third most obnoxious page—and since Chan's absent *snooty-fruity* Latina receptionist acted altogether indifferent to my presence in that office—I just got to my feet and promptly left."

§

Now the sole phrase out of these three compact paragraphs that impotent Creek cop Thompson could specifically quote as even remotely "threatening" was my rather unflattering depiction of Chan's receptionist as *"snooty-fruity."* Well, that's a descriptive adjective, not a "threat," and I'll repeat it here once more with emphasis—***SNOOTY-FRUITY***—as that's precisely how she conducted herself. So charge me with assault-to-commit-intentional-bodily-harm-with-a-deadly-descriptive-adjective!

That single, solitary legitimate visit to Chan's office took place last August 2007 at which time I never even met much less communicated with Chan—verbally or in writing by "letter" or telephone—before or since! Here my ominous memo copy arrives in mid-October 2007.

Obviously Chan was miffed my report named her office and figured she'd indulge in a splashy display of retaliatory harassment by making a patently bogus complaint to the cops about me, and I told Thompson as much.

Now it never ceases to amuse me when ever-defensive, ever-in denial cops lamely attempt to get pseudo-intellectual—latent pseudo-intellectuals as most invariably are—but Thompson then launched into this powerfully ludicrous and laughable lecture about how people's "perceptions" of what's "threatening" or "harassment" could so vastly differ.

Right! Now I'm prepared to submit the above aforementioned paragraphs concerning Chan's office to any court, any mass media outlet or for that matter any conceivable public forum whatever, and daresay challenge any rational and reasonably sane person of even exceptionally inferior intelligence to adjudge the first phrase contained therein as "threatening."

Well, as I told Thompson, I've got news: whilst I have absolutely no desire whatever to disrespect self-flattering Chan's preference to have no form of contact with me—the feeling's mutual though there was never any "threat" of that to start with, trust me!—I reserve the right to post any private business correspondence whenever I want to whomever I want. So long as it's not "inappropriate or illegal," Thompson cautioned me further. Who then decides that—him?

Well, I've got even more news: I'm promptly posting a follow-up report now to the Dental Board of California recounting exclusively Chan's lame attempt to exploit the local cops to harass me in response to the previous report posted—only this time, per her demand, I won't post any courtesy copy to her.

Clearly then Chan filed a patently false police report. And in Great Britain—if we're to believe certain Britcoms shown on PBS—she'd be rightly charged and arrested for the offense of "wasting police time." Why else couldn't she "relay" her own admonishments and warnings then rather than exploiting the cops to run her errands for her? And hadn't Thompson better things to do or just way too much time on his hands? "Swamped" with weeks'-old "cases," he admitted.

So, I questioned Thompson outright, is it the function of police to be the runners of complaining citizens? "That's your interpretation," he answered evasively, attempting lamely to be pseudo-intellectual again. It was a clear-cut question, not an interpretation. So taken aback about the entire matter I couldn't help but ask him outright: why the heck was he calling me in the first place? To "relay the message" for Chan he kept on repeating ridiculously. At his behest, not hers, I'd wager.

"We're a public service-oriented department," Thompson finally confided upon being pressed, boasting about all "this much time" he was granting me so generously in response to my questions, claiming he'd called me because the powers-that-be issuing his paycheck "expected" him to—otherwise had it been up to him he would've done "nothing." As well he should've done just that, most absolutely: nothing!

No crime was committed here. No "probable cause" even to suspect any crime committed existed here. Not even any rational "perception" of any crime committed conceivably existed here. Yet Thompson saw fit to contact me in his officious capacity as a Creek cop to "relay the message" of Chan's direct "threat" of arrest for "trespassing" upon her business property. Watch out, boy, Big Brother's watching you!

Well, quite frankly, my legitimate private business correspondence is none of the Creek police's freakin' business. And what with so many "progressive" police-avoided Bay Area neighborhoods being virtual ultra-violent war zones of rampant crime and mayhem—due primarily to criminally negligent deterrent police patrol and vigilance—this rather warped and unbelievably bizarre police priority, so obsessively preoccupied with my private legitimate business correspondence, rates its own report to the California Attorney General! And so it shall get it.

If anything **S. Chan** should've been arrested for filing a ***false police report*** per Walnut Creeks' own legal code:

"***Sec. 4-2.01.***

"*False Reports Unlawful.*

"*It shall be unlawful for any person knowingly to report or cause to be reported to the Police Department any false or fictitious request for protection or assistance, or any false or fictitious information indicating that a crime has been or is about to be committed, or to knowingly cause the Police Department to respond to any such false or fictitious report, or to request any assistance or investigation in connection with or as a result of any such false or fictitious report or false or fictitious information. (5520, as amended by §1, Ord. 1143, eff. August 30, 1972)"*

EPILOGUE:

OFFICER

DOWN,

SO

SHOULD

ANYBODY

CARE?

"We're not here to make any-body happy!" cracked the impotent Bay Area Rapid Transit(BART)cop, idling his do–nothing, good–for–nothing wiseass late Friday night the 11th of May 2001 at the so–called "downtown" Berkeley *Bog* BART station, where some bloated and equally wiseass BART agent gloated, "You're gonna be walking if you were planning to ride the last Fremont train."

All I'd done, you see, was simply approach the train station ticket turnstile—calmly and quietly going my own way and minding my own business—about to de-scend to the passenger platform below to await the ar-rival of the last Richmond–bound train, scheduled to depart at 12:52AM. I was headed for home in nearby El Cerrito after staying over late visiting my comely young Filipina girlfriend in the Berkeley *Bog*. Evidently a late Colma–bound train coming from the Pittsburg–Bay Point line caused the last Richmond–bound train's ar-rival and departure to be delayed until roughly 1:11AM.

In the San Francisco Bay Area the peninsula city of Colma lies south of the City and the distant land-locked city of Pittsburg is situated across the Bay in the westward Ygnacio Valley. Richmond is the north-ernmost destination on the BART line connecting the neighboring towns of Oakland, Berkeley and El Cerrito in the East Bay flats. Fremont, quite the contrary, is the southernmost destination in the diametrically opposite direction along the East Bay.

So here I came, entering the BART station simply to board the last Richmond–bound train and embark for home in nearby El Cerrito, getting inexplicably accost-ed by two smart–alecky and utterly useless jerk–offs.

Because of the public animosity and resentment

145

these habitually rude and obnoxious clods typically *provoke* it's small wonder every BART agent station box posts this ominous warning sign:

"PUBLIC NOTICE
ASSAULT OR BATTERY ON A STATION AGENT OR ANY BART EMPLOYEE IS PUNISHABLE BY IMPRISONMENT AND/OR FINES UP TO $10,000. CALIFORNIA PENAL CODE SECTIONS 243.3 AND 245.2"

§

"We're not here to make anybody happy!" is likely the mightiest understatement of the entire Millennium, but at the very same time, the most profoundly telling about the majority attitude that impotent cops harbor against most citizens they pretend to "serve and protect!"

Personally though I'd just *love* to square off for a little *legal* one–on–one with *any* willing impotent cop in a physical bout for the pure pleasure of it—*anytime.*

Realistically though most impotent power–tripping, control–freak cops are very much like lawless street gangs: both run in cowardly packs to prey upon those they perceive as too weak and powerless to fight back and defend themselves; both hide most cowardly behind weapons their victims can't or don't typically carry.

In a telling way impotent cops are far more cowardly and corrupt since they likewise hide behind badges and unequal laws, granting them unjust license and immunity to abuse and misuse their authority as well as to commit crimes forbidden to the rest of us.

If you most mistakenly think that's too harsh, or worse, most misguidedly swallow that crapola propaganda slogan about protecting and serving the community then just bend your brain a bit and ask yourself *honestly* these few simple questions:

•When was the last time you were *anyplace* ever served much less protected by an impotent cop?

•When was the last time you were ever *helped*—not harassed or hampered—by an impotent cop?

•When was the last time you ever met an impotent cop openly displaying even an *attitude* for helping much less protecting or serving you?

Rarely if at all, right? Well, then, I rest my case!

Typical episodes recounted in this book stress emphatically that this habitually ineffectual, inept and wasteful impotent cop conduct is the *rule*—not the exception!

In the meantime, cops whiningly complain they lack the funds and "manpower" to properly patrol the most dangerous and deadly of crime–ridden neighborhoods, yet *legions* of their most impotent shrimps magically materialize in *full force* to courageously confiscate the beer cans of peaceful revelers at public street festivals and parties. *Uncanny!*

What can the independent "alternative" and pretentiously progressive press do to make sure impotent crime–busting cops actually *earn* the respect they most misguidedly and most mistakenly think their badges, batons, guns and "laws" automatically entitle them to?

•Forget printing those sappy, juvenile ride–the–patrol–beat–for–a–day–with–a–cop–publicist articles.

•Analyze impotent cop logbook activity and incident reports for types of calls responded to and how disposed.

•Prioritize the truly serious crimes—assaults, burglaries, robberies, rapes and murders—impotent cops actually prevent and solve compared with the typically penny ante incidents they most habitually preoccupy themselves with wasting their time and effort on.

•Search out common citizens habitually bullied, intimidated or otherwise screwed over and victimized by corrupt impotent cops and print *their* stories! No doubt there's endless grist for the proverbial journalistic mill of the investigative brand.

If you witlessly persist and go on just pretending to be liberal–minded and progressive, failing to actually do something just a bit grown–up, meaningful and of some real and practical use to someone else for a refreshing change, then don't whine or complain when some impotent cop oppresses you, because sooner or later it'll most surely happen if it hasn't already.

§

On the internet is this website christened, ***The Officer Down Memorial Page, Inc.(ODMP), Remembering all of law enforcement's heroes***, *"a non–profit organization dedicated to honoring America's fallen law enforcement heroes. More than 19,000 officers have made the ultimate sacrifice in the United States and it is with great honor that the ODMP pays a lasting tribute to each of these officers by preserving their memories within its pages. All who visit the ODMP will be deeply moved by the countless stories of selfless courage and heroism exhibited by officers who lost their lives while serving and protecting the citizens of this great nation."*

In its "history" section the website puffs:

"By raising funds through tax deductible visitor contributions, the ODMP can continue to honor recent fallen heroes and support research to discover officers killed in the line of duty who have long since been forgotten.

"It is the hope of all those involved with the ODMP that each name added to the site will be the last. Until and after that day comes we are committed to honoring those souls who have made the ultimate sacrifice in the name of justice."

§

To counterbalance and offset such outright police puffery and propaganda there ought to exist an internet website devoted to all the countless unfortunate victims of ruthless and relentless police brutality and misconduct!

Impotent cops put on such a grandiose, grandstanding splashy display whenever one of their own gets killed or otherwise falls "in the line of duty."

Duty? Just how do most impotent cops discharge their sworn duty for the most part? Harassing couples peacefully parked together in perfectly legal spaces? Ticketing drivers parking temporarily in red curb zones which they themselves abuse to perform transactions at the very same nearby bank ATMS? Obsessively attempting to prove their exceptionally impotent and petty "points" by gloating whilst issuing the most trivial of traffic citations? Performing so–called "aggressive" deterrent and preventive patrol of known so–called "lovers' lanes" rather than equally well–known high violent crime–ridden neighborhood areas where people most routinely get assaulted, burglarized, robbed and murdered? Trumping up false charges against innocuous citizens for no other probable cause or reason except their perfectly legitimate and rightful "contempt–of–cop" attitude towards police? Spinelessly sitting on their craven, cowardly asses outside of their own dangerous jurisdictions looking for easy traffic ticket marks—too fucking afraid to enforce the "law" against the muggers, robbers and murderers in their own deliberately avoided neighborhoods? Bravely rousting students for missing bike lights or homeless people pushing shopping carts?

As this modest book with its consistent anecdotal evidence most tellingly suggests the list is endless and goes on and on in perpetuity.

So should anybody really much care when some impotent cop bites the dust?

Once I pause to seriously consider all the outright pain, suffering, agony, anguish, anxiety, distress, misery, torment, affliction, bother, difficulty and hardship these evil knaves and villains maliciously and viciously inflict upon the most innocuous of citizens on a daily, regular basis—over and over, time and time again, day in and day out, week after week, month after month, year after bloody year—then, no, I'm quite frankly not too terribly inclined to get too terribly bothered or broken up by it. Way I see it that's just one less impotent cop sadist abusing and mis–using his authority to make a misery the lives of the most harmless and helpless of citizens.

So my parting shots at the most impotent of those utterly useless penny ante police: if you're really out to be so gung–ho about discharging your duties, supposedly protecting and serving your community, then by God be a *MAN* and quit marking time on your shift looking for easy marks(like punk kids and the homeless)for proving your non–existent manhood! If you're too impotent to do your *JOB*, in short, then by God resign your commission and make way for somebody else who's capable, competent and can perform on the job! In any case find something to do that's *IMPORTANT* and just might *HELP* instead of hurt somebody on the street for a refreshing *CHANGE!*

Now I must be one amongst the most peaceful and so–called "law–abiding" persons on the planet—proved in part by my lack of any so–called "police record."

But I've had more than plenty enough distasteful and unpleasant encounters with the most impotent of your ilk to see right through you for the outright craven and dastardly chicken–shit cowards most of you really and truly are—hiding as you do behind your badge, baton, gun, and the "law" like a pansy, wimpy milquetoast hides behind some girl's skirts!

Likewise if now you're bent all out of shape and you've got some petty gripe or beef against me for writing the unvarnished truth about you in this book then again: *BE* a *MAN* and come after me *ALONE like* a *MAN*—leaving behind the badge, baton, gun, fellow gangsters and skirts of the "law" to confront me about it.

That is, of course, if you think you can actually *HACK IT being* a *MAN!*

In that context of defending myself against unpro-voked attack for expressing my constitutional rights of free speech and expression I'm always and ever more than ready and willing to take on *ANY* of you—*ANYTIME!* Then we can *really* see *what's what!*

Given your cowardly track record recounted so ac-curately in this book though, between you and me, we both know full well it'll never ever happen *that* way anytime soon if at all.

Be a *COP*—not an impotent *COWARD!*

Be a real *MAN* and the next time you're confront-ed with a contempt–of–cop citizen then preserve and protect the United States Constitution, which you're *SWORN* to do—*ALL* of it, including that part which you hate and detest most:

*"Congress shall make no law respecting an establishment of religion, or prohibiting the free exercise thereof; or abridging the **freedom of speech**, or of the press; or the right of the people peaceably to assemble, and to petition the Government for a redress of grievances."*

APPENDIX:

PROFESSIONS

OF

POLICE

PROPAGANDA,

LAW ENFORCEMENT CODE OF ETHICS,

LAW ENFORCEMENT OFFICER'S PLEDGE,

PEEL'S PRINCIPLES OF LAW ENFORCEMENT

LAW ENFORCEMENT CODE OF ETHICS

"As a law enforcement officer, my fundamental duty is to serve mankind; to safeguard lives and property; to protect the innocent against deception, the weak against oppression or intimidation, and the peaceful against violence or disorder; and to respect the constitutional rights of all men to liberty, equality and justice.

I will keep my private life unsullied as an example to all; maintain courageous calm in the face of danger, scorn, or ridicule; develop self-restraint; and be constantly mindful of the welfare of others. Honest in thought and deed in both my personal and official life, I will be exemplary in obeying the laws of the land and the regulations of my department. Whatever I see or hear of a confidential nature or that is confided to me in my official capacity will be kept ever secret unless revelation is necessary in the performance of my duty. I will never act officiously or permit personal feelings, prejudices, animosities or friendships to influence my decisions. With no compromise for crime and with relentless prosecution of criminals, I will enforce the law courteously and appropriately without fear or favor, malice or ill will, never employing unnecessary force or violence and never accepting gratuities.

I recognize the badge of my office as a symbol of public faith, and I accept it as a public trust to be held so long as I am true to the ethics of the police service. I will constantly strive to achieve these objectives and ideals, dedicating myself before God to my chosen profession...law enforcement."

Well, all I've got to say is: In 55 years of living I've yet to meet the first impotent cop who even remotely *attempted* to abide by his own frequently flouted code of ethics—quite the contrary to their fictional fantasy!

More often than not, impotent cops are out to harm and hamper rather than serve mankind; endangering rather than protecting lives and property with their overly reckless driving habits and irresponsible discharges of their weapons in all manner of circumstances and situations; omitting the truth and outright lying during interrogations to deceive, coerce false confessions under duress and otherwise incriminate and prosecute the innocent; harassing, intimidating and oppressing the weak(the homeless, impoverished and mentally ill in particular); provoking violence against the most peaceful and law–abiding of citizens; and violating the constitutional rights of peaceful protesters to speak out and express themselves freely with repressive and suppressive police actions and excessive force—acting especially officious, prejudicial and uncivil against all those citizens rightfully exercising their prerogative to hold "contempt–of–cop" attitudes.

And that's just the tip of the proverbial corrupt impotent cop iceberg!

LAW ENFORCEMENT OFFICER'S PLEDGE

"Be ready to serve the public faithfully and fearlessly 24 hours a day.
Uphold the right of every individual within the law.
Strive diligently to secure the evidence to free the innocent as well as convict the guilty.
Honor his badge—never tarnish it with personal misconduct, on or off duty.
Be courteous and friendly—for most citizens the only contact with law enforcement is to report or seek information.
Avoid favoritism—race, creed, and influence have no place on the scales of justice.
Act as a model to youth—help youngsters to be good citizens.
Keep in good physical condition. A healthy body and mind mean better work.
Learn more about the law enforcement profession—acquiring knowledge is a never–ending process.
Be loyal to self, organization, country and God."

www.ingramcontent.com/pod-product-compliance
Lightning Source LLC
Chambersburg PA
CBHW031515270326
41930CB00006B/406